AF316659

ACT NOW- OBJECTIVES & KEY RESULTS (OKRS)

ALIGN CONVERGE TAKE OFF

SRINIVAS MAHANKALI & VIKRAM KOHLI

In honor of those whose vision and leadership have shaped the world of goals and growth:

To **Andrew Grove**, Inventor of OKRs and a pioneer in strategic leadership at Intel. Your visionary approach continues to inspire generations.

To **Jon Doerr**, Author of "Measure What Matters" and advocate for goal-setting excellence. Your insights have transformed how organizations define success.

To the **Honorable** Prime Minister of India, For fostering a climate of entrepreneurship and innovation, Empowering businesses to thrive and contribute to global progress.

This dedication is a tribute to their enduring influence and commitment to excellence.

Contents

Contents

Foreword

Art of War says "strategy without tactics is the slowest route to victory and tactics without strategy is the noise before defeat." Having worked with SMEs and Fortune-500 companies across the world driving strategy execution and performance management for decades, I can totally agree with this.

Businesses across the globe are challenged with the need to set clear, actionable objectives and achieve them through disciplined execution. It is more critical than ever. My friend Srinivas along with his colleague has outlined in their book "ACT NOW: Objectives and Key Results" a comprehensive guide to mastering this essential skill. This book is not just a theoretical exposition, but a practical manual that brings the transformative power of the OKR framework to life.

I have had the pleasure of working with numerous organizations across industries, helping them navigate the complexities of strategic alignment and business transformation. One of the most common challenges I encounter is the gap between strategy formulation and execution. Many companies excel at setting ambitious goals, what we call BHAGs (Big Hairy Audacious Goals), but they often struggle to translate these goals into actionable tactics. Kaplan and Norton's Balanced Scorecard was the most preferred framework for this but most clients lacked the excellence and rigour demanded by the framework for measuring, monitoring and managing objectives at all levels. The OKR framework perhaps offers a less rigorous alternative to align individual goas to the strategy/

Srinivas Mahankali and Vikram Kohli bring a wealth of experience and expertise to the table. Srinivas, an IIT/IIM alumnus with over 35 years of executive experience, has a profound understanding of the strategic frameworks that drive business success. His extensive work in aligning strategies for profitable growth, coupled with his pioneering efforts in Blockchain and Web 3.0 technologies, makes him a leading voice in the field. Vikram, with his deep passion for building and scaling tech products, complements this expertise with his practical insights into product vision and execution.

Together, they have created a book that not only explains the principles of OKRs but also offers actionable steps to implement it effectively. Their approach emphasises the importance of aligning company objectives with measurable outcomes and actionable plans, imbibing a culture of discipline, and enhancing team collaboration. The book is rich with real-world examples, strategic tips, and best practices, making it a must0have resource for leaders at all levels.

"ACT NOW" will prompt CEOs and business leaders to embrace OKR for driving sustained growth. It equips them with the tools and knowledge to create focus, accountability, and high performance. By adopting the OKR framework as outlined in this book, they can ensure every team member is aligned with the company goals, driving collective success with clear line of sight.

I highly recommend this book to anyone looking to unlock their organization's full potential. It is a powerful guide that will inspire you to act with urgency, implement with precision, and achieve with excellence.

Dr M Muneer
Strategy Execution Expert, Fortune-500 advisor, Start-up Investor and Global Expert Columnist

Preface

In today's rapidly evolving business landscape, startups are emerging daily, each with ambitious dreams of disrupting industries and creating lasting impact. Meanwhile, established companies, despite their solid foundations, often find themselves grappling to sustain growth and adapt to the changing market dynamics. Through my extensive career working with numerous large organizations, I have observed a recurring challenge: a pervasive struggle to maintain focus and alignment with their stated mission. The lack of alignment and accountability across various levels within these organizations has frequently diluted their efforts to achieve their visions.

This book is born out of my experiences and observations from working closely with many such organizations. I have witnessed firsthand how the absence of a clear, structured approach to goal setting can drain organizational resources and hinder progress. However, amidst these challenges, I have also encountered a beacon of hope in the form of the OKR (Objectives and Key Results) system. Pioneered and successfully adopted by industry giants like Intel, Google, and Deloitte, the OKR framework offers a practical solution to catalyze an organization's journey towards success.

The inspiration to write this book stems from a deep-seated belief in the transformative power of OKRs. I have seen how this system can provide the clarity, focus, and alignment that many organizations desperately need. Through this book, I aim to share insights and practical guidance on how organizations—both startups and established companies—can implement the OKR system to drive growth and achieve their strategic goals.

Writing this book has been a journey in itself, marked by extensive research, numerous interviews with industry experts, and my own hands-on experience in implementing OKRs across various organizational settings. The process has been both challenging and enlightening, reinforcing my conviction in the efficacy of OKRs.

I bring to this book not just theoretical knowledge, but practical insights drawn from real-world applications. With a background in business management and years of experience in strategic consulting, I have had the privilege of working with some of the most dynamic and forward-thinking leaders in the industry. These experiences have equipped me with a unique perspective on what it takes to drive organizational success in today's complex business environment.

I also wish to thank my co-author Vikram Kohli, who is very passionate about leveraging OKRs for organizational success and has extensively worked in implementing the OKR system across several organizations during his stint at Qilo. His expertise and dedication have been invaluable in the creation of this book.

In sharing our journey and the lessons learned, we hope to provide readers with a valuable resource that not only explains the principles of OKRs but also offers actionable strategies for their successful implementation. Whether you are a startup founder looking to build a strong foundation or an executive in a large organization seeking to realign your team's efforts, this book is for you.

Thank you for joining us on this journey. We hope you find the insights and strategies shared within these pages to be both inspiring and practical, empowering you to lead

your organization towards a brighter, more focused future.
    Sincerely,
    Srinivas Mahankali

Acknowledgements

This book is the result of countless hours of research, interviews, and collaboration with experts in the field. I am deeply grateful to all those who have contributed their knowledge, experiences, and insights.

I wish to thank Mr Diwakar Ram Boddupalli who always triggered my inquisitiveness through intelligent discussions and pointing me to new approaches to unlocking human and organisational potential.

I wish to thank Dr Muneer Mohammed , the leading Management and Organisational excellence consultant in India, who has helped many organisations to Align for Growth.

Special thanks go to the pioneers of OKRs, whose vision and innovation have paved the way for countless organizations to achieve their goals.

Prologue

The Case for Implementing Corporate Alignment Strategies

Organizational alignment is a crucial driver of growth. Aligning strategy, culture, and talent can significantly impact a company's performance. This alignment is akin to the coordination of the three leadership cartoon characters pulling together to keep the profitable revenue growth arrow pointing onward and upward. Corporate alignment strategies like Balanced Scorecard and OKRs (Objectives and Key Results) provide a structured approach to achieving this alignment and driving organizational success.

The Job of Leaders in Creating Growth

Leaders play a pivotal role in fostering organizational alignment and driving profitable growth. While many businesses strive for profitable growth, aligning all critical factors to achieve consistent and highly profitable growth is challenging. However, organizational alignment is worth the effort.

Research conducted by 3x Organizational Alignment Research Model conducted on 410 companies across eight industries reveals that highly aligned companies:

Grow revenue 58% faster

Are 72% more profitable

Satisfy customers 3.2-to-1

Engage employees 16.8-to-1

These statistics underscore the significant benefits of achieving organizational alignment. When strategy, culture, and talent are aligned, companies experience faster growth, higher profitability, better customer satisfaction, and greater employee engagement.

The Cost of Organizational Misalignment

On the flip side, misalignment of strategy, talent, and culture leads to underperformance. For example:

PMI found that misaligned organizations lose an average of $109 million for every $1 billion spent on projects due to missed goals and budget overruns.

McKinsey's Organizational Health Index discovered that misaligned companies generate half the return on invested capital and 18% less in EBITDA.

IDC found that companies lose at least 10% of potential revenue growth from weak sales and marketing alignment.

These figures highlight the substantial costs associated with organizational misalignment. Misaligned organizations not only miss out on potential revenue but also face inefficiencies and reduced profitability.

Implementing Corporate Alignment Strategies

Corporate alignment strategies like the Balanced Scorecard and OKRs are essential tools for leaders seeking to achieve and maintain alignment within their organizations.

Balanced Scorecard: This strategy helps translate a company's vision and strategy into actionable objectives across four perspectives: financial, customer, internal processes, and learning and growth. By providing a comprehensive view of the organization's performance, the Balanced Scorecard ensures that all aspects of the business are aligned and contributing to strategic goals.

OKRs (Objectives and Key Results): OKRs offer a framework for setting ambitious objectives and measurable key results. This approach encourages stretch goals and fosters innovation while maintaining focus on critical outcomes. By regularly reviewing and adjusting OKRs, organizations can stay agile and responsive to changing conditions, preserving the entrepreneurial spirit.

Implementing corporate alignment strategies like the Balanced Scorecard and OKRs is essential for driving organizational growth and success. Highly aligned companies experience faster revenue growth, higher profitability, better customer satisfaction, and greater employee engagement. Conversely, misaligned organizations face significant costs and inefficiencies. By prioritizing alignment and leveraging these strategic frameworks, leaders can create a cohesive, high-performing organization that consistently achieves its goals and thrives in a competitive landscape.

The Genesis of OKRs: A Story of Transformation

In the relentless march of progress, the ability of organizations to adapt and innovate often determines their survival. As the business landscape evolves, so too must the strategies that drive it. Among the myriad methodologies that have emerged, Objectives and Key Results (OKRs) stand out for their simplicity, versatility, and profound impact. This book is a journey into the world of OKRs—a framework that has redefined goal-setting and performance management for some of the world's most successful companies.

The story of OKRs begins in the 1970s with Andy Grove, the visionary leader of Intel. Grove, a proponent of "management by objectives," recognized that the rapidly changing technology landscape required a dynamic and adaptive approach to goal-setting. He developed the OKR framework to ensure that Intel's strategic objectives could be translated into actionable, measurable results at every level of the organization. This system allowed Intel to navigate the complexities of the semiconductor industry and achieve unparalleled success.

The Rise of OKRs: From Silicon Valley to Global Adoption

The true potential of OKRs was unleashed when John Doerr, a venture capitalist and former Intel employee, introduced the framework to a fledgling company named Google in the early 2000s. Google's founders, Larry Page and Sergey Brin, embraced OKRs, embedding them into the fabric of their company's culture. The results were transformative. Google's meteoric rise from a startup to a global technology titan is a testament to the power of OKRs in driving focus, alignment, and execution.

Today, OKRs are not just the domain of tech giants. Companies across industries—from small startups to large enterprises—have adopted OKRs to foster innovation, enhance performance, and achieve strategic objectives. This widespread adoption underscores the universality and adaptability of the OKR framework, making it a valuable tool for organizations of all sizes and sectors.

Why This Book?

Despite the growing popularity of OKRs, many organizations struggle with their implementation. Misconceptions about the framework, lack of clear guidelines, and failure to integrate OKRs into the organizational culture often lead to suboptimal results. This book aims to demystify OKRs, providing a comprehensive guide to understanding, implementing, and leveraging the framework effectively.

Drawing on real-world examples, case studies, and practical insights, this book will equip you with the knowledge and tools needed to harness the full potential of OKRs. Whether you are a leader looking to drive strategic alignment, a manager seeking to improve team performance, or an individual contributor aspiring to achieve personal goals, this book will serve as your roadmap to success.

The Structure of This Book

The book is structured to provide a holistic understanding of OKRs, from their foundational principles to advanced implementation techniques. Each part of the book builds on the previous one, offering a logical progression of concepts and practical advice.

Introduction to OKRs

We begin with the basics, exploring the origins, philosophy, and fundamental components of the OKR framework. You will learn about the history of OKRs, their key influencers, and the core principles that underpin this powerful goal-setting system.

The Philosophy Behind OKRs

This section delves deeper into the underlying philosophy of OKRs. We will explore the importance of setting ambitious objectives, the power of measurable key results, and the benefits of adopting OKRs. By understanding the "why" behind OKRs, you will be better equipped to embrace and champion the framework within your organization.

Implementing OKRs

Effective implementation is crucial to the success of OKRs. In this section, we provide a step-by-step guide to implementing OKRs, from getting leadership buy-in to crafting effective objectives and key results. You will learn about the best practices for rolling out OKRs, integrating them into existing processes, and overcoming common challenges.

Managing and Reviewing OKRs

OKRs are not a set-it-and-forget-it system. Continuous tracking, review, and adaptation are essential to maintaining momentum and achieving results. This section covers the processes and tools needed to track progress, conduct regular reviews, and make data-driven adjustments to your OKRs.

Case Studies and Examples

Nothing illustrates the power of OKRs better than real-world examples. This section presents case studies from a diverse range of organizations, highlighting how OKRs have been successfully implemented to drive growth and innovation. You will gain insights into the practical application of OKRs across different industries and organizational contexts.

Advanced Topics in OKRs

For those looking to deepen their expertise, this section explores advanced topics such as integrating OKRs with other frameworks, scaling OKRs across large organizations, and leveraging technology to enhance OKR processes. We also discuss emerging trends and the future of OKRs in the evolving business landscape.

Resources and Tools

To support your OKR journey, we provide a range of resources and tools, including templates, worksheets, and a review of popular OKR software. This section also includes a curated list of further reading materials to help you expand your knowledge and stay updated on the latest developments in the field.

Conclusion

We conclude the book with a recap of key concepts, reflections on the ongoing journey of OKRs, and encouragement to start implementing the framework in your organization. The conclusion serves as a call to action, inspiring you to leverage OKRs to drive meaningful and sustainable success.

Who This Book is For

This book is designed for a wide audience, reflecting the broad applicability of the OKR framework:

Leaders and Executives: Learn how to align organizational goals with strategic priorities and foster a culture of accountability and transparency.

Managers and Team Leaders: Discover how to set effective team objectives, measure progress, and motivate your team to achieve ambitious targets.

Individual Contributors: Understand how to use OKRs to set personal goals, track progress, and contribute to the overall success of your organization.

Consultants and Coaches: Gain insights into the best practices for advising clients on OKR implementation and driving transformational change.

Final Thoughts

Embarking on the OKR journey is both exciting and challenging. It requires commitment, discipline, and a willingness to embrace change. However, the rewards are well worth the effort. By adopting OKRs, you can transform your organization, driving alignment, focus, and performance to new heights.

As you read this book, I encourage you to approach it with an open mind and a readiness to act. OKRs are more than just a framework—they are a mindset and a tool for achieving extraordinary results. I hope this book inspires you to take the first step on your OKR journey and empowers you with the knowledge and tools to succeed.

Welcome to the world of OKRs. Let's get started.

CHAPTER ONE

Introduction

"Highly aligned companies grow revenue 58% faster and are 72% more profitable than their less-aligned counterparts." — LSA Global Research

In today's fiercely competitive world, where new startups emerge daily and industries continually evolve, the demand for optimal utilization of resources and maximizing Return on Investment (ROI) has never been higher. Organizations are under immense pressure to deliver extraordinary returns on every dollar invested while navigating the complex landscape of competitive pressures.

Imagine a horse cart with multiple horses pulling it in different directions. The cart would be torn apart, failing to move effectively towards its destination. This analogy mirrors what happens in organizations when resources, including the human workforce, are not aligned with the overarching goals of the company. Just as the horses must pull together in the same direction, every element of an organization must work harmoniously towards a common objective to ensure success.

The Need for Alignment

Alignment within an organization is not just a nice-to-have; it is critical for survival and growth. The foundation of this alignment begins with the purpose of the organization. Purpose is an overarching statement that defines the "why" of the business. It encapsulates the fundamental reason for the organization's existence and what it seeks to accomplish. A clear purpose provides direction and inspires everyone within the organization to contribute towards a shared vision.

From Purpose to Strategy

The journey from purpose to execution involves several key steps, each requiring careful planning and alignment. Once the purpose is clearly defined, the next step is to create a strategy. Strategy involves identifying the key initiatives, actions, and resources necessary to achieve the North Star Metric—an ultimate measure of success that aligns with the organization's purpose. This strategy must be crafted with precision, ensuring that it stays true to the core values and long-term vision of the organization.

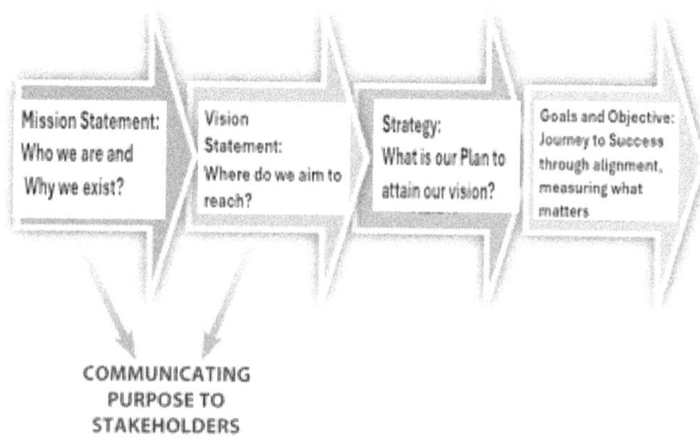

The Purpose to Goals : Need for Alignment and Execution Excellence

As CEOs, ensuring clarity across our organization's mission, vision, values, long-term goals, and yearly objectives is paramount. Simon SInek, the famous Management Guru and the author of 'Start with Why' gave a powerful framework with the 'Why What How' approach that re;ates to the Purpose , vision and Mission of many successful organisations across the globe.

The "Why, What, How" framework is a powerful tool for aligning an organization's activities with its vision and mission. Here's how each element relates to an organization and ties into its vision and mission:

<u>Why</u>

Purpose and Motivation: The "Why" represents the organization's core purpose and motivation. It answers the fundamental question of why the organization exists.

Vision Connection: This is directly related to the company's vision, which describes what the organization aspires to become in the long-term. The "Why" aligns with the vision by providing a clear reason for the organization's existence and the impact it aims to have on the world.

<u>What</u>

Goals and Objectives: The "What" defines what the organization aims to achieve. These are the specific goals and objectives that guide the organization's efforts.

Mission Connection: This is linked to the company's mission, which outlines what the organization does to achieve its vision. The "What" includes the concrete objectives and key results (OKRs) that help the organization fulfill its mission.

<u>How</u>

Methods and Processes: The "How" describes the methods, processes, and strategies the organization will use to achieve its goals. It details the approach and actions taken.

Operational Alignment: The "How" ensures that the daily operations, culture, and values of the organization are in sync with its mission and vision. This includes the implementation of strategic plans and the efficient execution of tasks.

Relationship with Vision and Mission

Vision: The vision provides the inspirational and aspirational "Why" that drives the organization forward. It sets the long-term destination.

Mission: The mission provides the actionable "What" that the organization needs to do to move towards its vision. It defines the organization's purpose and primary objectives.

Alignment: The "How" ensures that the organization's strategies, operations, and daily activities are aligned with both the vision and the mission, ensuring coherence and effectiveness.

In summary, the "Why, What, How" framework helps an organization align its purpose (Why) with its goals (What) and the methods to achieve them (How), all of which should be closely tied to the organization's vision and mission for cohesive growth and success.

Strategic management focuses on setting long-term goals, defining strategies to achieve them, and aligning resources accordingly. It prioritizes vision, direction setting, and decision-making that shapes the organization's future. Operational management, on the other hand, deals with day-to-day activities, ensuring efficient execution of plans, and achieving short-term objectives. Its priority lies in optimizing processes, managing resources, and ensuring the smooth functioning of daily operations to support strategic goals. Both layers are essential: strategic management provides overarching direction, while operational management ensures effective implementation to achieve strategic objectives.

Different Layers of Organisational Management

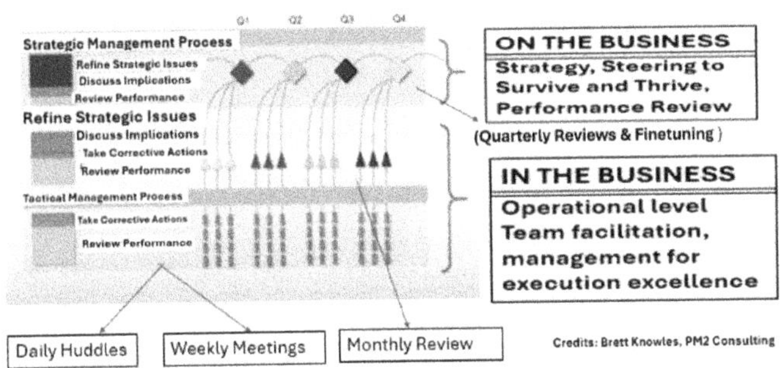

Key Layers of Management and their Priorities

OKRs serve as a powerful tool to translate our mission into aspirational annual objectives, reviewed quarterly or more frequently. Instead of solely asking "did we deliver what we planned?" each quarter, OKRs prompt us to ask "did we achieve the objectives we aimed for?" This shift in focus enables us to continually assess and adjust our strategic path.

OKR Approach: Empowering the Organisaiton for Execution Excellence

To effectively introduce OKRs, start by identifying three or four high-level objectives for the entire year at the CEO level. Each part of the organization then aligns their quarterly objectives to these overarching goals. This dual approach—setting ambitious yearly targets alongside quarterly milestones—facilitates organizational learning and highlights how each area contributes to our collective success.

Your objectives should support your mission and company values, while aligning closely with both long-term and short-term goals. To introduce OKRs effectively:

Set Annual Objectives at the CEO Level: Identify three or four objectives the organization aims to achieve over the year. This typically starts at the CEO level.

Cascade Objectives to Teams: Each part of the organization then identifies related objectives to achieve in each of the four quarters of the year. This method ensures that annual targets are broken down into manageable, quarterly goals, helping teams understand how their work contributes to the broader organizational objectives.

Focus on Measurable Key Results: It is crucial to identify measurable key results to track progress towards objectives. If key results are only measurable annually, it limits the ability to assess progress and make timely adjustments. Given the increasing pace of change, annual assessments are insufficient.

OKRs provide a proven system for organizations to advance towards their annual goals and long-term vision. However, it is essential that team OKRs align with the company's mission and higher-level goals. This alignment does not imply that team OKRs are dictated from above. Instead, it means that company goals and the overall mission are communicated effectively and understood clearly before teams set their specific OKRs.

By ensuring that team-level OKRs are aligned with the company's mission and goals, organizations can foster a unified direction, improve focus, and enhance the likelihood of achieving their strategic objectives.

By embedding OKRs into our strategy, we empower our teams to focus on impactful outcomes that drive continuous progress and success.

Tactical Goals and Operations

Strategic objectives are often broad and long-term. To translate these into actionable steps, organizations must establish tactical goals. These are short-term objectives that provide insight into proposed innovations, differentiations, and key projects. Tactical OKRs (Objectives and Key Results) are set by functions, departments, business units, or specially formed cross-functional teams. They break down the broader strategy into manageable, measurable components that can be executed in the near term.

Operational OKRs and initiatives, on the other hand, define day-to-day and frequent operational activities. This is where the rubber meets the road. Teams closely execute these activities, providing regular progress updates to tactical and strategic OKRs. Operational activities are often detailed and task-oriented, focusing on immediate outputs and efficiencies.

Continuous Alignment for Success

For an organization to perform at its best and ensure success, there must be continuous alignment across all levels—from purpose to strategy to tactics and operations. This alignment ensures that every action taken within the organization contributes meaningfully to the overarching goals, driving performance and achieving desired outcomes.

This is where the concept of OKRs comes into play. OKRs provide a structured framework that helps organizations maintain this alignment, fostering a culture of focus, accountability, and transparency. By setting clear objectives and measurable key results, OKRs ensure that every team and individual within the organization understands their role in achieving the collective goals. This alignment is not a one-time effort but an ongoing process of setting, tracking, and reviewing goals to ensure sustained success.

Convergence and Energy

Alignment leads to convergence, and convergence leads to the unlocking of tremendous internal energy within the organization. This unified effort channels the collective capabilities and passion of the workforce towards achieving the company's goals. Imagine a magnifying glass focusing the energy of the sun's rays to burn a hole in a piece of paper. Similarly, when an organization's resources are aligned and converge towards a singular objective, they can achieve extraordinary results, igniting progress and innovation.

The focused energy within an organization can drive remarkable transformations. Instead of diffused efforts that lead to mediocre outcomes, convergence through OKRs allows for the concentration of efforts, enabling teams to tackle challenges with precision and vigor. This focused approach can accelerate growth, enhance productivity, and create a resilient organization capable of thriving in competitive environments.

Embracing OKRs for Extraordinary Results

OKRs have been embraced by some of the world's most successful companies, from tech giants like Google to innovative startups across various industries. The power of OKRs lies in their simplicity and adaptability, making them an effective tool for driving performance and achieving extraordinary results. By fostering a disciplined approach to goal-setting and execution, OKRs enable organizations to navigate the complexities of the modern business environment and thrive amidst competition.

In this book, we will explore the principles, practices, and real-world applications of OKRs. You will learn how to implement OKRs effectively within your organization, ensuring that every team member is aligned with the purpose, strategy, and tactical goals. Through practical insights and case studies, you will gain a deep understanding of how OKRs can transform your organization, driving alignment, focus, and exceptional performance.

Join us on this journey to discover how OKRs can help you achieve your most ambitious goals and lead your organization to extraordinary success. Keep a 'Magnifying glass' handy...

The Origin of OKRs

Introduction

The OKR (Objectives and Key Results) framework is now widely recognized as a powerful tool for driving organizational alignment and performance. However, to appreciate its full potential, it's essential to understand the history and evolution of OKRs. This chapter delves into the origins of OKRs, tracing their roots back to early management theories and examining their development into the robust system used by leading companies today.

Early Management Theories and Goal-Setting

The foundation of OKRs can be traced back to the early 20th century when management theories began to emerge, focusing on efficiency and goal-setting. Frederick Winslow Taylor's scientific management and Henri Fayol's administrative theory laid the groundwork for structured goal-setting and performance measurement. Taylor's time and motion studies, for example, emphasized the importance of setting clear objectives to improve productivity.

Around the same time, the concept of Management by Objectives (MBO) was being developed. Peter Drucker, often referred to as the father of modern management, introduced MBO in his 1954 book, "The Practice of

Management." MBO emphasized setting clear, achievable objectives and aligning them with organizational goals. Although MBO was revolutionary, it had limitations, such as a lack of flexibility and difficulty in adapting to rapidly changing business environments.

The Birth of OKRs

The transition from MBO to OKRs began in the late 1960s and early 1970s with Andrew Grove, the co-founder of Intel. Grove, a student of Drucker's work, saw the need for a more dynamic and agile goal-setting framework. He recognized that the rapidly evolving technology sector required a system that could adapt quickly to change and drive alignment across the organization.

In his 1983 book, "High Output Management," Grove introduced a goal-setting methodology that would later become known as OKRs. The essence of Grove's system was to set clear objectives (the "O") and define measurable key results (the "KRs") that would indicate progress towards those objectives. This approach was designed to be simple, flexible, and transparent, addressing many of the shortcomings of MBO.

Objectives and Key Results Defined

To understand the innovation that Grove brought with OKRs, it's crucial to break down the two components:

Objectives: These are clear, concise statements that define what you aim to achieve. Objectives should be ambitious yet achievable, providing a sense of direction and motivation.

Key Results: These are specific, measurable outcomes that indicate progress toward the objective. Each objective typically has three to five key results, ensuring that progress can be tracked and measured. Key results should be quantifiable and time-bound.

Intel's Implementation of OKRs

Intel's implementation of OKRs revolutionized the company's performance management. Grove's methodology encouraged a culture of transparency, accountability, and alignment. By setting clear objectives and measurable key results, Intel was able to align its workforce, drive focus on critical priorities, and foster a performance-oriented culture.

One of the key advantages of OKRs was their flexibility. Unlike the rigid annual goals of MBO, OKRs were set and reviewed quarterly, allowing Intel to adapt to changes in the market and technology landscape swiftly. This adaptability was crucial in the fast-paced semiconductor industry.

The Spread of OKRs: From Intel to Silicon Valley

The success of OKRs at Intel did not go unnoticed. As Intel became one of the leading technology companies in the world, other companies in Silicon Valley began to take note of its innovative goal-setting framework. The most notable adoption of OKRs outside Intel came from Google.

In the early days of Google, John Doerr, a venture capitalist from Kleiner Perkins who had previously worked with Intel, introduced OKRs to Google's founders, Larry Page and Sergey Brin. Doerr's presentation on OKRs resonated with Google's vision and culture. Google adopted OKRs and has used them ever since to drive its growth and innovation.

At Google, OKRs played a pivotal role in scaling the company from a small startup to a global technology giant. The framework provided a clear structure for setting ambitious goals and measuring progress, fostering a culture of transparency and accountability. Google's success story further popularized OKRs, and the framework began to spread to other tech companies and beyond.

The Evolution of OKRs

Since their adoption by Intel and Google, OKRs have continued to evolve. Today, they are used by a diverse range of organizations, from startups to multinational corporations, across various industries. The flexibility and simplicity of OKRs make them adaptable to different organizational contexts and goals.

One of the significant evolutions in OKRs has been the integration of technology. Modern OKR software solutions provide tools for setting, tracking, and reviewing OKRs, making the framework more accessible and easier to implement. These tools often include features for real-time feedback, collaboration, and analytics, enhancing the effectiveness of OKRs.

Principles of Effective OKRs

To fully leverage the potential of OKRs, organizations need to adhere to several key principles:

Transparency: OKRs should be visible to everyone in the organization. This transparency fosters accountability and ensures that everyone is aligned with the overall goals.

Alignment: OKRs should align with the organization's strategic objectives. This alignment ensures that every team and individual is working towards common goals, driving synergy and collaboration.

Ambition: Objectives should be ambitious, pushing the organization to stretch its capabilities and achieve more. However, they should also be realistic and achievable.

Focus: OKRs should be limited in number to ensure that the organization remains focused on its most critical priorities. Typically, each team or individual should have no more than five objectives.

Regular Review: OKRs should be reviewed regularly, typically on a quarterly basis. This regular review cycle allows for adjustments and ensures that progress is tracked continuously.

The Impact of OKRs on Organizational Culture

OKRs do more than just drive performance; they also have a profound impact on organizational culture. By fostering a culture of transparency, accountability, and continuous improvement, OKRs help create an environment where employees are motivated and engaged.

Transparency: When OKRs are visible to everyone, it creates a culture of openness and trust. Employees understand how their work contributes to the organization's goals and can see the progress being made across the organization.

Accountability: OKRs establish clear expectations and measurable outcomes. This clarity fosters accountability, as employees know what is expected of them and can track their progress.

Continuous Improvement: The regular review and adjustment of OKRs promote a culture of continuous improvement. Organizations can quickly identify areas for improvement and make necessary adjustments, driving ongoing performance enhancements.

Engagement: OKRs provide employees with a clear sense of purpose and direction. When employees understand the organization's goals and how their work contributes to achieving them, they are more likely to be engaged and motivated.

Case Studies: Successful OKR Implementations

Organizational Level:

Google: Google is one of the earliest and most well-known adopters of OKRs. At the organizational level, Google sets ambitious objectives such as improving user experience across all products or expanding into new markets. Each objective is supported by key results that are measurable and time-bound, aligning the entire organization towards strategic goals.

Intel: Andrew Grove, the creator of OKRs, implemented them at Intel to drive strategic focus and alignment. Intel used OKRs to guide major initiatives like developing new processor technologies or entering new segments of the semiconductor market, ensuring alignment with long-term business objectives.

LinkedIn: LinkedIn has also successfully implemented OKRs to drive its growth and innovation. The company uses OKRs to align its teams around strategic priorities and measure progress towards its goals. This alignment has been crucial in LinkedIn's journey from a startup to a leading professional networking platform.

Department Level:

Sales Department at Salesforce: Salesforce uses OKRs extensively to align their sales teams with corporate goals. For example, a sales department may set objectives around increasing revenue by a certain percentage, improving customer retention rates, and expanding into new markets. Key results could include metrics like closed deals, customer satisfaction scores, and market penetration rates.

Marketing Department at HubSpot: HubSpot's marketing department utilizes OKRs to enhance lead generation, brand awareness, and customer engagement. Objectives may focus on launching successful marketing campaigns, increasing website traffic, and improving conversion rates. Key results could measure leads generated, social media engagement metrics, and marketing-qualified leads (MQLs).

Team Level:

Product Development Team at Airbnb: Airbnb's product development teams use OKRs to innovate and improve user experience. Objectives might include enhancing platform usability or launching new features. Key results could track user feedback scores, feature adoption rates, and product release timelines.

Engineering Team at Spotify: Spotify's engineering teams align their efforts with OKRs to deliver technical solutions that support business growth. Objectives may involve optimizing system performance, reducing downtime, or enhancing scalability. Key results could measure server uptime, response times, and successful deployment frequency.

Product Development Team at Zynga: The gaming company Zynga adopted OKRs to drive its product development and innovation. By setting clear objectives and measurable key results, Zynga has been able to focus its efforts on creating engaging and successful games.

Individual Level:

Customer Support at Zendesk: Zendesk uses OKRs at the individual level within customer support teams. Objectives may revolve around improving customer satisfaction scores, reducing ticket resolution times, and increasing first-call resolution rates. Key results could track customer feedback ratings, ticket closure rates, and employee training completion.

Finance Team at Airbnb: Airbnb's finance team sets OKRs to improve financial forecasting accuracy, optimize budget allocation, and reduce operational costs. Objectives may focus on achieving financial targets, improving reporting processes, and ensuring regulatory compliance. Key results could include revenue forecasts accuracy, cost-saving initiatives implemented, and audit findings resolved.

These case studies illustrate how OKRs can be effectively applied at different organizational levels to drive alignment, focus, and performance towards achieving strategic objectives. Each example showcases how clear goal-setting and measurable outcomes contribute to organizational success and growth.

Challenges and Misconceptions

Despite their effectiveness, OKRs are not without challenges. Some common misconceptions and challenges include:

Overly Ambitious Goals: While ambition is important, setting unrealistic goals can be demotivating. Organizations need to strike a balance between ambition and achievability.

Lack of Alignment: If OKRs are not aligned with the organization's strategic objectives, they can lead to fragmented efforts and reduced effectiveness.

Infrequent Reviews: Regular review and adjustment are crucial for OKRs to be effective. Infrequent reviews can result in misalignment and reduced performance.

Overcomplication: OKRs should be simple and straightforward. Overcomplicating the framework can lead to confusion and reduced effectiveness.

The Future of OKRs

The future of OKRs looks promising as more organizations recognize the value of this framework in driving performance and alignment. As technology continues to evolve, OKRs are likely to become even more integrated with organizational processes, leveraging data and analytics to enhance goal-setting and tracking.

Moreover, the principles of OKRs are increasingly being applied beyond traditional business settings. Non-profits, educational institutions, and government agencies are adopting OKRs to drive performance and achieve their missions.

Conclusion

The journey of OKRs from their origins in early management theories to their adoption by leading companies like Intel and Google highlights the enduring value of this framework. OKRs provide a structured yet flexible approach to goal-setting, driving alignment, focus, and extraordinary results. As organizations continue to navigate the complexities of the modern business environment, OKRs offer a powerful tool for achieving success and unlocking their full potential.

In the following chapters, we will explore the practical aspects of implementing OKRs, share best practices, and provide real-world examples to help you leverage OKRs effectively in your organization. By understanding the origins and principles of OKRs, you will be better equipped to drive alignment, performance, and innovation in your organization.

CHAPTER THREE

Understanding OKRs

Introduction

As a CEO, you're constantly seeking ways to drive growth, improve efficiency, and foster innovation within your organization. OKRs (Objectives and Key Results) provide a structured yet flexible framework to help you achieve these goals. In this chapter, we will break down the concept of OKRs, explain why they are important, and show you how they can transform your organization's performance. We'll also integrate the concepts of FACTS (Focus, Align, Commit, Track, Stretch) and CFR (Continuous Conversation, Feedback, and Recognition) to provide a comprehensive understanding of OKRs.

What Are OKRs?

OKRs stand for Objectives and Key Results. It's a goal-setting framework that helps organizations define and track their objectives and the outcomes they need to achieve those objectives.

The OKR Formula

We will __________ as measured by __________ .
objective   these key results

Quantive

Enter Caption

Objectives: These are what you want to achieve. They should be clear, inspiring, and actionable. Objectives set the direction and focus for your organization.

Objectives are not expected to be a laundry list of strategic outcomes and also not long period bets, like five year plans for example. The value of your company objectives is inversely proportional to the number of pages required to express it. Your Company Objectives should be based on your • The strategic bets you are chasing • Your competitive landscape, • Technological & market condition changes. • And above all, what all it will take to enhance your product/service & company to be more customer-centric

Key Results: These are how you will measure the achievement of your objectives. Key results are specific, measurable, and time-bound metrics that track progress towards your objectives.

Imagine your objective is to "Increase customer satisfaction." Your key results might include "Improve Net Promoter Score (NPS) from 50 to 70," "Reduce customer support response time to under 2 hours," and "Achieve a 90% customer satisfaction rate in post-service surveys."

<u>**FACTS - CFR: The key dimensions of OKR implementation**</u>

OKRs are important because they bring several benefits to your organization, which can be encapsulated in the FACTS framework:

Focus: By setting a limited number of ambitious objectives, OKRs help your organization concentrate on what truly matters. This focus drives better results and prevents teams from being spread too thin.

Align: OKRs align the efforts of every team and individual with the organization's overall goals. This ensures that everyone is working towards the same objectives, reducing wasted effort and increasing efficiency.

Commit: OKRs require a commitment from all levels of the organization. This commitment fosters a culture of accountability where everyone is dedicated to achieving the set objectives.

Track: Regular tracking of key results helps in monitoring progress and making necessary adjustments. This ensures that the organization stays on course and can respond quickly to any challenges or changes.

Stretch: OKRs should be ambitious and challenging. Stretch goals push the organization to go beyond its comfort zone, driving innovation and extraordinary performance.

How Do OKRs Work?

To understand how OKRs work, let's break down the process into simple steps:

Set Objectives: Start by defining clear and ambitious objectives for your organization. These should be aligned with your long-term vision and strategic goals. For example, if your strategic goal is to become the market leader, your objective might be to "Increase market share."

Define Key Results: Once you have your objectives, identify the key results that will measure progress towards those objectives. These should be specific and measurable. For the objective "Increase market share," key results might include "Achieve 25% market share by the end of Q4," "Launch three new products," and "Expand into two new geographic markets."

Align and Cascade: Ensure that the objectives and key results are aligned across all levels of the organization. This means that departmental and team OKRs should support the overall organizational OKRs. For example, the marketing team's OKRs might include "Increase brand awareness by 30%" to support the objective of increasing market share.

Track and Review: Regularly track progress towards the key results. This involves frequent check-ins, reviews, and updates to ensure that you stay on track. At the end of the quarter, review the results and assess what worked and what didn't. This helps in learning and improving for the next cycle.

Celebrate and Iterate: Celebrate achievements and learn from any shortcomings. Use the insights gained to refine and improve your OKRs for the next cycle. This iterative process helps in continuously driving performance and innovation.

Integrating CFR: Continuous Conversation, Feedback, and Recognition

To maximize the effectiveness of OKRs, it's crucial to integrate Continuous Conversation, Feedback, and Recognition (CFR) into your OKR process:

Continuous Conversation: Regular communication ensures that everyone is on the same page and any issues are addressed promptly. This involves ongoing dialogues between managers and employees about progress, challenges, and priorities.

Feedback: Constructive feedback helps teams and individuals understand what they are doing well and where they need to improve. Feedback should be timely and specific, aligned with the progress towards key results.

Recognition: Recognizing achievements and efforts motivates employees and reinforces a culture of high performance. Celebrating wins, no matter how small, boosts morale and encourages a positive, productive work environment.

Real-World Examples

Let's look at how some leading companies have successfully implemented OKRs:

Google: Google has been using OKRs since its early days. One of their famous OKRs was set by the Chrome team with the objective to "Create the world's fastest browser." Their key results included "Achieve a 1-second page load time" and "Increase user base to 20 million." This OKR helped focus the team's efforts on speed and user adoption, contributing significantly to Chrome's success.

Intel: As the birthplace of OKRs, Intel used this framework to drive significant growth and innovation. An example of an Intel OKR might be "Launch the next-generation microprocessor." Key results could include "Complete design by Q2," "Achieve a 20% performance improvement," and "Reduce manufacturing cost by 15%."

LinkedIn: LinkedIn has used OKRs to scale its platform and enhance user engagement. An example objective might be "Increase user engagement." Key results could include "Grow active user base by 10%," "Increase content sharing by 25%," and "Improve user retention rate to 85%."

Common Pitfalls and How to Avoid Them

While OKRs are powerful, they can be challenging to implement effectively. Here are some common pitfalls and tips to avoid them:

Setting Too Many Objectives: Having too many objectives can dilute focus and overwhelm teams. Stick to a few high-impact objectives (typically 3-5) to maintain focus.

Vague Key Results: Key results should be specific and measurable. Avoid vague or qualitative key results that are difficult to track. Ensure that key results are clearly defined and can be objectively measured.

Lack of Alignment: Ensure that all OKRs are aligned with the overall strategic goals of the organization. This alignment ensures that every effort is contributing to the bigger picture.

Infrequent Reviews: Regular reviews are essential for tracking progress and making necessary adjustments. Schedule frequent check-ins and reviews to keep OKRs on track.

Resistance to Change: Change can be challenging, and some employees may resist the adoption of OKRs. Communicate the benefits clearly, provide training, and involve employees in the process to gain buy-in.

Implementing OKRs in Your Organization

Here's a step-by-step guide to implementing OKRs in your organization:

Educate and Train: Start by educating your leadership team and employees about OKRs. Provide training on how to set effective OKRs and the benefits of the framework.

Pilot Program: Begin with a pilot program in one or two departments. This allows you to refine the process and address any challenges before a full-scale rollout.

Set and Align OKRs: Work with teams to set and align their OKRs with the organizational goals. Ensure that everyone understands how their work contributes to the overall objectives.

Regular Check-Ins: Schedule regular check-ins to review progress and address any issues. These check-ins should be short and focused on tracking key results and making necessary adjustments.

Review and Iterate: At the end of the OKR cycle, conduct a thorough review. Assess what worked, what didn't, and why. Use these insights to improve the process for the next cycle.

Celebrate Successes: Celebrate achievements and recognize the hard work of your teams. This helps in building a positive culture around OKRs and motivates employees to strive for excellence.

OKRs offer a powerful framework for driving alignment, focus, and performance in your organization. By setting clear objectives and measurable key results, you can ensure that every effort is aligned with your strategic goals, fostering a culture of transparency, accountability, and continuous improvement.

As a CEO, your leadership is crucial in successfully implementing OKRs. By championing this framework and involving your teams in the process, you can unlock the full potential of your organization and drive extraordinary results. Remember to incorporate the principles of FACTS (Focus, Align, Commit, Track, Stretch) and CFR (Continuous Conversation, Feedback, and Recognition) to ensure the effectiveness and sustainability of your OKR process. In the next chapters, we will delve deeper into the practical aspects of setting, tracking, and reviewing OKRs, providing you with the tools and insights needed to leverage OKRs effectively.

CHAPTER FOUR

OKRs versus other Goal Setting Systems

In the quest for excellence, organizations often turn to various goal-setting frameworks to drive performance and achieve strategic objectives. Among these, OKRs (Objectives and Key Results) stand out due to their unique approach and numerous benefits. This chapter will delve into the differences between OKRs and other leading goal-setting systems, highlighting the unique propositions that make OKRs a preferred choice for many innovative and high-performing organizations.

<u>Traditional Goal-Setting Systems</u>

Before we explore the unique proposition of OKRs, it's essential to understand the traditional goal-setting systems commonly used by organizations. These include SMART Goals, Balanced Scorecard, Management by Objectives (MBO), and KPIs (Key Performance Indicators).

<u>SMART Goals:</u>

Specific: Goals should be clear and specific.

Measurable: Goals should have measurable outcomes.

Achievable: Goals should be realistic and attainable.

Relevant: Goals should align with broader business objectives.

Time-bound: Goals should have a clear timeframe.

Balanced Scorecard:

Focuses on four perspectives: Financial, Customer, Internal Processes, and Learning & Growth.

Aims to provide a comprehensive view of organizational performance.

Emphasizes balancing short-term and long-term objectives.

Management by Objectives (MBO):

Involves setting specific, measurable goals collaboratively with employees.

Emphasizes aligning individual objectives with organizational goals.

Includes regular performance reviews and feedback.

Key Performance Indicators (KPIs):

Quantitative metrics used to gauge performance.

Often focused on financial and operational aspects.

Used to track progress towards strategic goals.

OKRs: A Modern Approach

OKRs differ from these traditional goal-setting systems in several ways. Here are the unique propositions that set OKRs apart:

Ambition and Stretch Goals:

Unlike SMART goals that emphasize attainability, OKRs encourage setting ambitious and aspirational goals. These stretch goals push teams to go beyond their comfort zones and drive innovation and extraordinary performance.

Transparency and Alignment:

OKRs are typically shared across the organization, promoting transparency. This openness ensures that everyone understands the company's priorities and how their work contributes to the overall objectives, fostering alignment and a sense of shared purpose.

Frequent Review and Adaptation:

OKRs are set and reviewed on a quarterly basis, promoting agility and responsiveness. This frequent review cycle allows organizations to adapt to changing circumstances and recalibrate their goals as needed, ensuring continuous alignment with strategic priorities.

Focus on Outcomes, Not Activities:

OKRs emphasize outcomes (Key Results) rather than activities. This focus ensures that teams are driving meaningful results and not just completing tasks, leading to more impactful performance.

Integration of CFR (Continuous Conversation, Feedback, and Recognition):

The CFR model complements OKRs by fostering continuous dialogue and feedback. This integration ensures that progress is regularly discussed, achievements are recognized, and course corrections are made promptly.

Simplicity and Clarity:

OKRs are designed to be simple and easy to understand. The clear structure of Objectives and Key Results ensures that goals are straightforward and the path to achieving them is clear, reducing complexity and confusion.

OKRs vs. SMART Goals

Ambition: While SMART goals emphasize realistic and attainable goals, OKRs encourage setting stretch goals that challenge the organization to achieve more.

Frequency: SMART goals are often set annually, whereas OKRs are typically set quarterly, allowing for more frequent adjustments and alignment.

Transparency: OKRs promote organizational transparency by making goals visible to everyone, unlike SMART goals, which may not always be shared across the organization.

OKRs vs. Balanced Scorecard

Scope: The Balanced Scorecard focuses on balancing performance across multiple perspectives (financial, customer, internal processes, learning & growth), while OKRs emphasize ambitious objectives and measurable key results.

Frequency: Balanced Scorecards are usually reviewed annually, whereas OKRs are reviewed quarterly, promoting agility.

Transparency: OKRs are typically more transparent, encouraging alignment across the organization, while Balanced Scorecards may not always be as widely communicated.

OKRs vs. Management by Objectives (MBO)

Ambition: MBO focuses on achievable goals set collaboratively with employees, while OKRs encourage setting ambitious, stretch goals.

Frequency: MBO often involves annual goal-setting and reviews, whereas OKRs are set and reviewed quarterly, promoting continuous alignment and adaptation.

Focus: OKRs emphasize outcomes (Key Results) rather than activities, ensuring that the focus remains on driving meaningful results.

OKRs vs. Key Performance Indicators (KPIs)

Scope: KPIs are specific metrics used to measure performance, often focusing on financial and operational aspects. OKRs encompass broader organizational objectives and key results.

Integration: OKRs integrate KPIs as key results but go beyond by setting ambitious objectives and fostering alignment and transparency across the organization.

Frequency: KPIs are typically reviewed periodically (monthly or quarterly), while OKRs are set and reviewed quarterly, ensuring continuous alignment with strategic priorities.

The Unique Proposition of OKRs

The unique proposition of OKRs lies in their ability to drive focus, alignment, and ambitious performance through a transparent and agile framework. Here's a summary of what makes OKRs unique:

Ambitious Goals: OKRs encourage setting stretch goals that push the organization to achieve more, driving innovation and extraordinary performance.

Transparency: OKRs promote organizational transparency by making goals visible to everyone, fostering alignment and a sense of shared purpose.

Agility: The quarterly review cycle of OKRs ensures that organizations can quickly adapt to changing circumstances and recalibrate their goals as needed.

Outcome Focus: By emphasizing outcomes (Key Results) rather than activities, OKRs ensure that teams are driving meaningful results.

Simplicity: The clear and straightforward structure of OKRs makes goal-setting and tracking easy to understand and implement.

Integration of CFR: The Continuous Conversation, Feedback, and Recognition model complements OKRs, fostering continuous dialogue, feedback, and recognition, which are crucial for sustained high performance.

Conclusion

OKRs offer a modern and dynamic approach to goal-setting that addresses the limitations of traditional systems. By encouraging ambition, promoting transparency, fostering alignment, and ensuring agility, OKRs enable organizations to drive performance and achieve strategic objectives effectively. The integration of the CFR model further enhances the effectiveness of OKRs by fostering a culture of continuous improvement and recognition. As you consider implementing OKRs in your organization, keep in mind these unique propositions that set OKRs apart and position your organization for success in an ever-changing business landscape.

CHAPTER FIVE

KPIs and OKRs

Key Performance Indicators (KPIs) are quantifiable metrics used to evaluate the success of an organization, employee, project, or process in meeting objectives for performance. KPIs provide targets for teams to shoot for, milestones to gauge progress, and insights that help people across the organization make better decisions.

KPIs are an important component of the Organizational Goal Setting Process.

Alignment with Strategic Goals:

KPIs as a Measurement Tool: KPIs are directly tied to an organization's strategic goals. They are used to measure how well the organization is achieving its overall objectives. For instance, if a strategic goal is to increase market share, relevant KPIs might include sales growth, customer acquisition rates, or market penetration.

Cascade from Objectives: High-level organizational goals cascade down into specific objectives for departments and teams. KPIs are then defined at each level to ensure that every part of the organization is aligned and contributing to these strategic goals.

Focus and Prioritization:

Setting Priorities: KPIs help organizations prioritize their efforts by focusing on the most critical areas that will drive success. They highlight which aspects of performance are most important to monitor and improve.

Resource Allocation: By identifying key areas of performance, KPIs help in the allocation of resources (time, money, personnel) to areas that will have the greatest impact on achieving organizational goals.

Performance Monitoring and Evaluation:

Ongoing Assessment: KPIs provide a continuous feedback loop, enabling organizations to monitor progress toward their goals in real-time. This ongoing assessment helps in identifying issues early and making necessary adjustments.

Benchmarking and Accountability: KPIs establish benchmarks for performance and hold teams accountable for achieving them. Regularly tracking KPIs ensures that teams stay focused on their targets and are aware of how their work contributes to broader organizational goals.

Decision-Making and Strategy Adjustment:

Informed Decisions: KPIs provide data-driven insights that inform strategic decisions. Leaders can make better choices based on measurable performance indicators rather than intuition alone.

Adapting Strategies: When KPIs indicate that performance is not meeting expectations, organizations can adjust their strategies. This flexibility allows organizations to stay agile and responsive to changes in the market or internal dynamics.

Motivation and Engagement:

Clear Targets: Clear and achievable KPIs give employees concrete targets to aim for, increasing motivation and engagement. Employees understand how their work contributes to organizational success.

Recognition and Rewards: KPIs can be tied to performance appraisals, recognition programs, and incentives. When employees meet or exceed their KPIs, it can lead to rewards and recognition, further driving motivation and performance.

KPIs are integral to organizational goal setting as they provide a measurable way to track progress towards strategic objectives, ensure alignment across the organization, and drive focus, accountability, and continuous improvement. By effectively leveraging KPIs, organizations can enhance performance, make informed decisions, and achieve their long-term goals.

Relationship Between KPIs and OKRs

KPIs (Key Performance Indicators) and OKRs (Objectives and Key Results) are both tools used to measure and manage performance within an organization, but they serve different purposes and have distinct characteristics. Here's how they are related and how KPIs can complement Key Results:

Key Differences and Complementary Roles:

Purpose and Scope:

OKRs: Used for setting ambitious goals and aligning efforts across the organization. Objectives are qualitative, while Key Results are specific, measurable outcomes that indicate progress toward the objective.

KPIs: Used to measure ongoing performance and operational efficiency. KPIs are typically more stable and track performance over time.

Time Frame:

OKRs: Often set on a quarterly or annual basis, focusing on specific, time-bound objectives.

KPIs: Monitored continuously and can be tracked on a daily, weekly, monthly, or annual basis.

<u>Focus:</u>

OKRs: Aim to drive change and improvement, focusing on achieving significant, often transformative goals.

KPIs: Focus on maintaining and improving current performance and ensuring the organization operates efficiently.

How KPIs Complement Key Results:

Measuring Progress:

Alignment: KPIs can serve as benchmarks or indicators of progress toward Key Results. For example, if an Objective is to increase customer satisfaction, a relevant KPI might be the Net Promoter Score (NPS), which helps measure progress towards this Key Result.

Granularity: While Key Results provide high-level targets, KPIs offer detailed, ongoing measurements that can signal whether the organization is on track to achieve these results.

Informing OKR Setting:

Baseline Data: KPIs provide historical performance data that can inform the setting of realistic and ambitious Key Results. Understanding current performance levels through KPIs helps in defining achievable yet challenging OKRs.

Performance Gaps: KPIs highlight areas of underperformance that may become focal points for future OKRs. For instance, if a KPI indicates low employee engagement, an OKR might be set to improve this metric.

Continuous Feedback Loop:

Monitoring and Adjustment: KPIs offer real-time feedback that can help in adjusting efforts to achieve Key Results. Regular KPI reviews can identify issues early, allowing teams to course-correct and stay on track with their OKRs.

Validation: Successful achievement of Key Results can often be validated through KPIs. If a Key Result is to reduce customer churn by 10%, the corresponding KPI will show the actual churn rate and confirm whether the Key Result has been met.

Operational Efficiency and Strategic Goals:

Balancing Act: While OKRs drive strategic initiatives and ambitious goals, KPIs ensure that operational efficiency and day-to-day performance are maintained. Together, they provide a balanced approach to managing both strategic and operational aspects of the business.

Resource Allocation: KPIs help in identifying where resources are currently being used effectively and where they might be reallocated to better support the achievement of OKRs.

Example:

Objective: Improve Customer Satisfaction

Key Result 1: Increase Net Promoter Score (NPS) from 40 to 60.

Key Result 2: Reduce average customer response time from 24 hours to 12 hours.

Complementary KPIs:

Customer Support KPIs: Number of support tickets, response time, resolution time.

Customer Feedback KPIs: NPS, Customer Satisfaction Score (CSAT), Customer Effort Score (CES).

In this example, KPIs like response time and NPS directly measure the progress of the Key Results and provide continuous data to monitor and guide efforts.

Summary

KPIs and OKRs are both crucial for organizational success but serve different roles. OKRs set ambitious goals and drive strategic initiatives, while KPIs monitor ongoing performance and operational efficiency. When used together, KPIs can complement Key Results by providing detailed, continuous measurements that inform, validate, and guide the achievement of strategic objectives.

The 4 Pillars of OKR approach

In today's dynamic business environment, achieving strategic alignment and maintaining a laser focus on key objectives are crucial for organizational success. The Objectives and Key Results (OKR) system has emerged as a powerful framework to address these needs, driving performance, accountability, and continuous improvement. The OKR system is built on four foundational pillars: Values, Principles, Phases, and Elements. Each pillar plays a vital role in ensuring that the OKR framework is not just a set of goals, but a comprehensive approach to strategic execution and organizational growth.

Values form the core beliefs that underpin the OKR system, emphasizing clarity, alignment, transparency, engagement, and intrinsic motivation. These values ensure that every individual understands the objectives, is aligned with the organizational goals, and is motivated by personal growth and contribution.

Principles guide the application of the OKR framework within an organization. They emphasize focus, agility, continuous improvement, short iterations, and self-organizing teams. These principles ensure that the organization remains adaptable, prioritizes critical goals, and fosters a culture of constant learning and innovation.

Phases outline the stages of the OKR process, from defining the vision to setting interim goals, establishing objectives, determining key results, and implementing initiatives and actions. These phases provide a structured approach to translating high-level aspirations into actionable and measurable outcomes.

Elements are the components that support the functioning of the OKR system. They include roles like the OKR Champion, tools such as the OKR List, processes like retrospectives and planning & review sessions, and the cadence of ceremonies that maintain the rhythm of the OKR cycle. These elements ensure that the system operates smoothly, promotes accountability, and drives continuous progress.

Together, these four pillars create a robust framework that helps organizations set ambitious goals, track progress, adapt to changes, and continuously improve. By embracing the OKR system, organizations can achieve greater alignment, foster a culture of high performance, and drive sustained success in an ever-evolving business landscape.

The values, principles, phases, and elements that form the backbone of an effective OKR system, ensuring it drives alignment, clarity, and continuous improvement in your organization are outlined below.

1. OKR Values

Clarity

Clarity is the bedrock of the OKR system. It ensures that everyone within the organization understands what the objectives are and what key results are necessary to achieve them. This clarity is vital for effective communication, preventing misunderstandings, and aligning team efforts. When objectives and key results are clear, every team member knows exactly what is expected, which tasks are priorities, and how their work contributes to the broader organizational goals.

Alignment

Alignment ensures that all efforts within the organization are synchronized towards common goals. This is crucial in preventing siloed efforts where different departments or teams work on projects that don't contribute to the overall strategy. With proper alignment, individual and team objectives are interconnected and support the broader organizational goals, creating a cohesive effort towards shared success. This alignment can be achieved through cascading OKRs, where top-level objectives inform the objectives of subsequent levels within the organization.

Transparency

Transparency promotes openness and visibility across the organization. It means that everyone has access to the OKRs, can see what others are working on, and understands how their efforts fit into the larger picture. Transparency fosters trust, accountability, and a culture of shared responsibility. When employees know that their progress is visible to everyone, they are more likely to stay committed to their goals and take ownership of their work.

Engagement

Engagement is about involving every team member in the goal-setting and achieving process. Engaged employees are more likely to be committed to their objectives, put in extra effort, and take initiative. Engagement is fostered by involving employees in the creation of their OKRs, ensuring they have a voice in setting their goals and understanding how their work contributes to the organization's success. This ownership leads to higher motivation and productivity.

Intrinsic Motivation

Intrinsic motivation refers to the internal drive that propels individuals to achieve their goals for personal satisfaction and growth, rather than external rewards. The OKR system aims to cultivate intrinsic motivation by setting meaningful and challenging goals that inspire employees. When employees see their work as valuable and aligned with their personal and professional growth, they are more likely to be motivated and perform at their best.

2. OKR Principles

Focus

Focus is about concentrating on a few critical objectives rather than spreading efforts across too many goals. The OKR system encourages setting a limited number of objectives (typically 3-5) to ensure that teams can dedicate their full attention and resources to achieving them. This focus helps prevent burnout, increases the likelihood of success, and ensures that the most important goals receive the necessary effort and resources.

Agility

Agility in the OKR system allows organizations to adapt quickly to changing circumstances. By setting shorter cycles (quarterly or even monthly), the OKR framework provides the flexibility to pivot and adjust objectives and key results in response to new information or shifts in the market. This agility ensures that the organization remains relevant and can seize opportunities or mitigate risks promptly.

Continuous Improvement

Continuous improvement is a core principle of the OKR system. It promotes a culture of ongoing learning, experimentation, and refinement. Regularly reviewing and reflecting on OKR progress helps teams identify what works, what doesn't, and how to improve in the next cycle. This iterative process of setting, tracking, and reviewing OKRs fosters a mindset of constant enhancement and growth.

Short Iterations

Short iterations refer to the practice of setting and reviewing OKRs within brief, manageable periods, usually quarterly. These short cycles provide frequent opportunities to assess progress, make adjustments, and celebrate achievements. They help maintain momentum, keep goals relevant, and ensure that the organization can respond swiftly to any changes or challenges that arise.

Self-Organizing Teams

Self-organizing teams are empowered to take ownership of their OKRs and determine how best to achieve them. This principle fosters autonomy, creativity, and accountability. When teams are trusted to organize their work, they are more likely to be innovative and find efficient solutions. This empowerment also increases engagement and satisfaction, as team members feel more in control of their success.

<u>3. OKR Phases</u>

Vision

The vision is the long-term aspiration or mission that guides the organization's strategic direction. It is the overarching purpose that provides context and meaning to the OKRs. A clear and inspiring vision motivates employees and aligns their efforts towards a common future. The vision should be ambitious yet attainable, providing a north star that guides all strategic initiatives.

Interim Goals

Interim goals are milestones or shorter-term targets that help bridge the gap between the vision and the immediate objectives. These goals provide a roadmap for achieving the long-term vision, breaking it down into manageable, actionable steps. They help maintain focus and momentum by offering checkpoints to measure progress and make necessary adjustments along the way.

Objectives

Objectives are specific, actionable goals that an organization aims to achieve within a defined period, typically a quarter. They are qualitative and set the direction for what needs to be accomplished. Effective objectives are ambitious, inspiring, and clearly articulated. They should challenge the organization to stretch its capabilities and drive significant progress towards the vision.

Key Results

Key results are the measurable outcomes that indicate progress towards the objectives. They are quantitative and provide a clear benchmark for success. Each objective typically has 3-5 key results that track performance and ensure that the objective is on track to being achieved. Key results should be specific, time-bound, and challenging yet achievable. They provide a clear framework for assessing progress and making data-driven decisions.

Initiatives and Actions

Initiatives and actions are the specific tasks and activities undertaken to achieve the key results. They are the execution steps that turn objectives and key results into reality. These initiatives should be well-defined, actionable, and aligned with the key results. Regular tracking and adjustment of these actions ensure that they remain relevant and effective in driving progress towards the objectives.

4. OKR Elements

OKR Champion

The OKR Champion is a person responsible for driving the OKR process within the organization. This role involves providing guidance, support, and ensuring adherence to the OKR framework. The OKR Champion acts as a coach and facilitator, helping teams set effective OKRs, track progress, and conduct regular reviews. They play a crucial role in fostering a culture of accountability and continuous improvement.

OKR List

The OKR List is a comprehensive compilation of all the objectives and key results within the organization. It provides a clear overview of what each team and individual is working towards and how these efforts align with the overall strategy. The OKR List should be easily accessible and regularly updated to ensure transparency and alignment across the organization.

Retrospective

A retrospective is a review process where teams reflect on their OKRs, evaluate what worked well, identify challenges, and determine areas for improvement. This practice fosters a culture of learning and continuous improvement. Regular retrospectives help teams understand their successes and failures, learn from their experiences, and make informed adjustments for future OKR cycles.

Planning & Review

Planning and review sessions are regular meetings where teams set new OKRs and review progress on existing ones. These sessions ensure that OKRs remain relevant, aligned with the overall strategy, and reflective of any changes in the organizational environment. They provide an opportunity for teams to discuss challenges, celebrate achievements, and realign efforts as needed.

Ceremonies & Cadences

Ceremonies and cadences refer to the scheduled meetings and checkpoints that maintain the rhythm and discipline of the OKR process. These can include weekly check-ins, monthly reviews, quarterly planning sessions, and annual strategy meetings. These regular touchpoints ensure that progress is tracked, challenges are addressed promptly, and the organization remains focused and aligned towards its goals.

Conclusion

The OKR system is a powerful framework for driving strategic alignment, clarity, and continuous improvement within an organization. By adhering to its values, principles, phases, and elements, organizations can create a structured yet flexible approach to goal-setting and achievement. The OKR system fosters a culture of transparency, engagement, and intrinsic motivation, empowering teams to focus on what matters most and adapt swiftly to changing circumstances. Regular review and reflection ensure that the organization remains on track towards its vision, continuously improving and evolving in response to new challenges and opportunities. By embracing the OKR system, organizations can unlock their full potential, achieve ambitious goals, and drive sustained success.

CHAPTER SEVEN

Hierarchy of OKRs

The concept of Objectives and Key Results (OKRs) is a powerful framework used by organizations to set, track, and achieve their goals. At its core, OKRs foster alignment, engagement, and accountability across all levels of an organization. The hierarchical structure of OKRs is central to their effectiveness, ensuring that everyone in the organization is working towards common objectives while maintaining clarity and focus at each level of the organization.

OKRs consist of two main components:

Objectives: Qualitative goals that describe what you want to achieve. Objectives are ambitious, inspirational, and time-bound.

Key Results: Quantitative measures that indicate how you will achieve the objective. Key results are specific, measurable, and verifiable.

Together, these components drive an organization's strategic vision down to actionable tasks and measurable outcomes.

The Need for a Hierarchical Structure

In large and complex organizations, such as conglomerates, the hierarchical structure of OKRs ensures that strategic goals set at the top level are effectively translated into operational goals at lower levels. This hierarchy is crucial for several reasons:

Alignment: Ensures that every team and individual are aligned with the organization's overall strategic direction.

Focus: Helps in maintaining focus on key priorities at each level of the organization.

Clarity: Provides clear and measurable goals that are relevant to each team and individual, making it easier to track progress and make adjustments.

Engagement: Engages employees by connecting their work to the broader organizational goals, enhancing motivation and accountability.

The Levels of OKR Hierarchy

Group-Level OKRs:

Purpose: Set the strategic direction and long-term goals for the entire organization or conglomerate.

Scope: Broad and encompassing, addressing the overall mission and vision of the organization.

Examples: Increasing market share, enhancing sustainability, achieving financial growth.

Business Unit-Level OKRs:

Purpose: Translate group-level strategic goals into specific objectives for each business unit.

Scope: Focused on the unique priorities and challenges of each business unit.

Examples: Launching new products, entering new markets, improving operational efficiency.

Department/Division-Level OKRs:

Purpose: Break down business unit objectives into actionable goals for individual departments or divisions.

Scope: Tailored to the functions and responsibilities of each department.

Examples: Enhancing customer service, reducing production costs, improving product quality.

Team-Level OKRs:

Purpose: Further break down department-level goals into specific objectives for teams and enhance the transparency, collaboration and communication among teams..

Scope: Focused on team-specific tasks and projects.

Examples: Completing a project on time, achieving a sales target, developing a new feature.

Individual-Level OKRs:

Purpose: Align personal goals with team, department, and business unit objectives.

Scope: Personalized and relevant to each employee's role and responsibilities.

Examples: Improving individual performance metrics, developing new skills, completing specific tasks.

General Timelines for OKR Cycles

OKRs are typically set and reviewed on specific timelines to ensure regular progress and adjustments:

Annual Planning:

Set at the beginning of the fiscal year.

Defines long-term strategic objectives at the group and business unit levels.

Quarterly Planning:

Set at the beginning of each quarter.

Breaks down annual objectives into manageable quarterly goals at the department, team, and individual levels.

Weekly Check-Ins:

Conducted weekly to review progress, identify obstacles, and make necessary adjustments.

Ensures continuous alignment and focus on priorities.

Mid-Quarter Reviews:

Conducted halfway through each quarter.

Assess progress and realign efforts as needed.

Quarter-End Reviews:

Conducted at the end of each quarter.

Evaluate performance, celebrate achievements, and plan for the next quarter.

Benefits of a Hierarchical OKR Structure

The hierarchical structure of OKRs offers several benefits:

Strategic Alignment:

Ensures that all levels of the organization are working towards common goals.

Creates a clear line of sight from top-level objectives to individual contributions.

Focused Execution:

Helps maintain focus on the most important priorities at each level.

Prevents teams and individuals from being overwhelmed by conflicting goals.

Enhanced Accountability:

Makes it clear who is responsible for achieving specific goals.

Encourages ownership and accountability at all levels.

Increased Engagement:

Connects employees' daily work to the organization's broader mission and vision.

Enhances motivation and engagement by showing how individual efforts contribute to overall success.

Agility and Flexibility:

Allows for regular review and adjustment of goals based on progress and changing circumstances.

Encourages a proactive approach to addressing challenges and seizing opportunities.

Understanding the hierarchical structure of OKRs is essential for effectively implementing this powerful framework in any organization, particularly in complex, multi-level conglomerates. By ensuring alignment, focus, and accountability across all levels, the hierarchical approach to OKRs drives cohesive execution and helps organizations achieve their strategic objectives. With clearly defined timelines for setting and reviewing OKRs, organizations can maintain agility and responsiveness, ultimately leading to sustained success and growth.

CHAPTER EIGHT

What stage are you in?

Different organisations are at different stages with respec to the implementation of OKRs. It is importnat for orgnisations to introspect and target the desired level with corresponding stretched time lines.

To explain the stages of implementing OKRs (Objectives and Key Results) in an organization, let's break down the process into four distinct stages as shown in the images:

Stage 1: No Shared Goals

Characteristics:

No clear goals: At this stage, the company has not established clear goals beyond basic targets such as revenue and customer growth.

Lack of reviews: There are no regular monthly or quarterly reviews of progress and impact.

Reactive roadmap: The company's roadmap is reactive, with new projects being decided only after current ones are completed.

Micro-management: Progress requires micro-management because the team lacks a clear understanding of the path forward.

Disengagement: The team feels disengaged from the product, as they are merely following directives from leadership without a sense of ownership or direction.

Signs:

Goals are limited to basic revenue and customer growth targets.

Absence of regular reviews of progress and impact.

The project roadmap is reactive rather than proactive.

The need for micro-management to make progress.

The team feels disconnected from the product and their work.

Context: In the early stages of a business, it's common to lack a well-defined view of future goals. The company is still figuring things out, trying to understand the market by talking to as many customers as possible. Metrics might exist, but they are not detailed or understood by the team.

Stage 2: We Want Goals

Characteristics:

Emerging awareness: The company starts to actively think about its long-term vision or North Star.

Initial metrics: Some metrics beyond basic targets are tracked, but they are mostly defined by leadership.

Key Performance Indicators (KPIs): The company begins covering KPIs like Monthly Active Users (MAUs), conversion rates, and Customer Acquisition Costs (CAC), but without specific improvement goals.

Quarterly reviews: Progress is generally reviewed on a quarterly basis.

Shared understanding: The team has a shared understanding of business vitals, but individuals may not feel they can make an impact.

Signs:

Metrics beyond sales and customer targets are present but defined by leadership.

KPIs are tracked but not yet goal-driven.

Quarterly reviews of progress.

A general shared understanding of business vitals.

Team members do not yet feel empowered to make significant impacts.

Context: As the company grows, it becomes challenging to maintain open discussions about the future with everyone. There's a need to build trust and become more data-driven. The focus is on defining a clearer direction and establishing a culture of goal-setting.

Stage 3: We Set Goals

Characteristics:

Goal-setting culture: The company has teams running workshops to define how they'll measure success.

Clear vision: Leadership provides a clear vision that guides the team.

Autonomy: Teams work autonomously, setting their own goals and reporting outcomes to leadership.

Structured goals: Goals are set each quarter and documented.

Tracking issues: Some goals are too ambitious, leading to big misses, and updates are sometimes missed.

Signs:

Champions of SMART goals and OKRs emerge.

Teams can define their own goals within the leadership's vision.

Ambitious targets sometimes lead to significant misses.

Goals are documented quarterly.

Inconsistent progress tracking.

Context: This stage marks the transition to scaling operations effectively. Teams start defining success metrics and working independently, though they still face challenges in tracking goals consistently. The focus shifts to refining goal-setting and ensuring alignment.

Stage 4: We Track Goals

Characteristics:

Outcome-driven: The company is driven by outcomes, with teams self-evaluating and making decisions based on progress.

Innovative solutions: Teams produce innovative solutions to achieve outcomes.

High engagement: Team members are highly engaged and accountable for their decisions.

Long-term focus: Leadership can focus on longer-term goals while teams handle quarterly outcomes.

Regular monitoring: Progress is shared and monitored regularly, and historical data is maintained.

Signs:

Familiarity with KPIs, SMART goals, and OKRs is widespread.

Teams can set and achieve significant improvement goals.

Leadership focuses on long-term goals.

Regular progress monitoring.

Historical data tracking to understand progress over time.

Context: At this mature stage, the organization fully embraces outcome-driven strategies. Teams have the autonomy and accountability to drive progress, resulting in high engagement and innovative problem-solving. Leadership can concentrate on strategic, long-term goals while teams manage quarterly objectives.

The journey from having no shared goals to effectively tracking and achieving them involves significant cultural and operational changes. Each stage represents a step towards building a goal-oriented, autonomous, and high-performing organization. The implementation of OKRs helps structure this evolution, ensuring alignment, engagement, and continuous improvement.

CHAPTER NINE

Types of OKRs

OKRs (Objectives and Key Results) can be categorized into three main types: Strategic, Tactical, and Operational. Each type serves different purposes and has distinct characteristics in terms of level, focus, direction, duration, and impact.

Strategic OKRs provide the broad, long-term vision and direction for the organization, ensuring alignment and focus on significant objectives that span across multiple years.

Tactical OKRs break down the strategic objectives into specific, actionable goals for departments or teams, typically reviewed on a quarterly basis to drive mid-term performance.

Operational OKRs focus on the short-term tasks and activities that individual team members or small teams need to accomplish to support the tactical OKRs, often reviewed monthly to ensure immediate impact and continuous progress.

<u>Strategic OKRs</u>

Level: Top-tier organizational level

Focus: Long-term vision and overarching goals

Direction: Top-down (set by senior leadership and aligned across the organization)

Duration: Annual or multi-annual (1-3 years)

Impact: High impact on the overall direction and success of the organization

Characteristics: Strategic OKRs are designed to align the entire organization towards a common vision and mission.

These OKRs are typically broad and ambitious, aiming to drive significant change or progress.

They provide a clear direction for the company, ensuring all teams and departments are working towards the same long-term objectives.

Example: "Expand market presence in Asia by 25% over the next two years."

<u>Tactical OKRs</u>

Level: Departmental or team level

Focus: Mid-term goals and specific departmental initiatives

Direction: Bi-directional (collaboration between leadership and department heads/team leaders)

Duration: Quarterly or bi-annual

Impact: Moderate impact, driving departmental performance and supporting strategic OKRs

Characteristics: Tactical OKRs translate the strategic objectives into specific, actionable goals for departments or teams.

These OKRs are more detailed and focus on achieving measurable outcomes within a shorter timeframe.

They ensure that each department or team understands its role in contributing to the organization's long-term objectives.

Example: "Increase the marketing team's lead generation by 15% within the next quarter."

<u>Operational OKRs</u>

Level: Individual or small team level

Focus: Short-term tasks and immediate operational activities

Direction: Bottom-up (set by team members with guidance from team leaders, aligned with higher-level OKRs)

Duration: Monthly or quarterly

Impact: Direct impact on daily operations and short-term performance

Characteristics: Operational OKRs are highly specific and granular, focusing on the day-to-day tasks and activities necessary to achieve tactical OKRs.

These OKRs are often more numerous and detailed, allowing for precise tracking and management of progress.

They empower individual team members to take ownership of their contributions to the overall objectives.

Example: "Improve customer response time by 10% in the next month."

Comparison Across Characteristics

Characteristic	Strategic OKRs	Tactical OKRs	Operational OKRs
Level	Organizational	Departmental/Team	Individual/Small Team
Focus	Long-term vision	Mid-term goals	Short-term tasks
Direction	Top-down	Bi-directional	Bottom-up
Duration	Annual/Multi-annual	Quarterly/Bi-annual	Monthly/Quarterly
Impact	High	Moderate	Direct/Immediate

Differnt Types of OKRs

Each type of OKR plays a crucial role in the overall success of the organization, ensuring that there is a clear link between daily activities and long-term goals. This hierarchical approach to OKRs helps maintain alignment, accountability, and focus at all levels of the organization.

CHAPTER TEN

Key stakeholders in implementing OKRs

The successful implementation of OKRs (Objectives and Key Results) in an organization hinges on the clear definition and diligent execution of specific roles. These roles ensure that the OKR framework is not only adopted but also ingrained into the company's culture, driving sustained focus and alignment across all levels of the organization. Properly assigned OKR roles help in maintaining the momentum of OKR cycles, facilitating regular reviews, and fostering a culture of accountability and transparency.

Implementing OKRs is a strategic endeavor that requires buy-in from the top leadership and active participation from every level of the organization. The roles involved in the OKR process can be broadly categorized into leadership roles, program management roles, and team roles. Each role carries distinct responsibilities that collectively contribute to the seamless execution and continuous improvement of the OKR framework.

<u>Facilitators of OKR paradigm in an organisation:</u>
Leadership Roles:

CEO/Executive Sponsor: The CEO or executive sponsor is the primary advocate for OKRs, ensuring that the framework aligns with the company's strategic vision and goals. This role involves setting the tone for the importance of OKRs, providing necessary resources, and fostering a culture that supports transparency and accountability.

Senior Leadership Team: The senior leadership team, including department heads and functional leaders, is responsible for setting and communicating top-level OKRs. They play a crucial role in ensuring that their respective teams understand and commit to the objectives and key results that align with the company's overarching goals.

Roles of Key Stakeholders in OKR Implementation

1. OKR Sponsor / OKR Program Management Head: This person is ultimately responsible for the adoption of the OKR initiative within the company

Role: The OKR Sponsor is typically a senior executive or a member of the leadership team who champions the adoption of OKRs throughout the organization. They provide strategic direction, support, and resources necessary for successful implementation.

Responsibilities:

Setting Vision: Articulate the vision and strategic objectives that OKRs will help achieve.

Securing Resources: Allocate budget, technology, and human resources needed for OKR implementation.

Overcoming Obstacles: Remove barriers and address organizational resistance to ensure OKRs are embraced at all levels.

Communicating Benefits: Communicate the benefits of OKRs to stakeholders, emphasizing alignment with business goals and driving performance improvement.

Example: The CEO of a company decides to implement OKRs to improve transparency and alignment across departments. They allocate funds for OKR software and initiate communication sessions to explain the benefits of OKRs to employees.

2. OKR Champion:

Role: The OKR Champion is a dedicated advocate for OKRs within the organization. They typically lead the OKR implementation efforts, working closely with teams to ensure OKRs are effectively adopted and integrated into daily operations.

Responsibilities:

Leading Implementation: Develop and execute the OKR implementation strategy and roadmap.

Training and Support: Provide training sessions, workshops, and resources to educate employees on OKR methodology and best practices.

Monitoring Progress: Track OKR adoption, provide guidance to teams, and ensure alignment with organizational goals.

Driving Accountability: Encourage accountability by holding regular OKR review meetings and fostering a culture of transparency.

Example: The Head of Operations serves as the OKR Champion, leading the rollout of OKRs across departments. They conduct training sessions, establish OKR guidelines, and monitor progress to ensure teams are aligned with company objectives.

3. OKR Program Lead/ OKR Program Management Manager: This individual is responsible for executing the tasks required to make the OKR implementation successful.

Role: The OKR Program Lead is responsible for overseeing the day-to-day management and execution of the OKR program. They coordinate activities, facilitate communication, and ensure consistency in OKR implementation across the organization.

Responsibilities:

Coordinating Activities: Plan and coordinate OKR setting cycles, reviews, and adjustments.

Facilitating Communication: Serve as a central point of contact for OKR-related inquiries and updates.

Providing Guidance: Offer guidance and support to teams on OKR methodology, setting ambitious yet achievable objectives, and defining measurable key results.

Evaluating Effectiveness: Monitor OKR performance, collect feedback, and make recommendations for continuous improvement.

Example: The HR Manager takes on the role of OKR Program Lead, overseeing the rollout of OKRs across all departments. They schedule OKR review sessions, facilitate communication between teams, and assess the impact of OKRs on employee engagement.

4. OKR Consultant:

Role: An OKR Consultant is an external advisor or expert who provides specialized knowledge and guidance on OKR implementation. They bring industry best practices, benchmarks, and insights to optimize OKR processes within the organization.

Responsibilities:

Providing Expertise: Offer expert advice on OKR framework, methodology, and implementation strategies tailored to the organization's needs.

Training and Workshops: Conduct training sessions and workshops to educate stakeholders on OKR fundamentals and advanced practices.

Benchmarking Performance: Benchmark OKR performance against industry standards and recommend adjustments for continuous improvement.

Troubleshooting: Address challenges and provide solutions for complex OKR issues that arise during implementation.

Example: A management consultant specializing in performance management is hired to advise on OKR implementation. They conduct a readiness assessment, design OKR frameworks, and provide ongoing support to ensure successful adoption.

Team Leaders and Managers: Team leaders and managers play a pivotal role in cascading OKRs down to their teams, aligning team objectives with company goals, and conducting regular check-ins and reviews. They are responsible for mentoring their team members in the OKR process and ensuring accountability.

Individual Contributors: Every team member is responsible for contributing to the achievement of OKRs. They need to understand how their work aligns with the broader organizational goals and regularly update their progress on key results.

<u>Importance of Stakeholder Roles in OKR Implementation</u>

Alignment: Stakeholders ensure OKRs are aligned with strategic goals and organizational priorities.

Support: They provide resources, guidance, and leadership needed to implement OKRs effectively.

Engagement: Stakeholders foster buy-in, engagement, and accountability among employees throughout the OKR journey.

Continuous Improvement: Their oversight and support enable continuous evaluation and refinement of OKR processes for optimal performance outcomes.

In summary, each stakeholder—whether as a Sponsor, Champion, Program Lead, or Consultant—plays a crucial role in guiding OKR implementation, ensuring alignment with strategic objectives, and driving organizational success through improved performance and accountability.

Defining these roles clearly and ensuring that the right people are assigned to each role is the first step towards a successful OKR implementation. It builds a solid foundation for fostering a culture of disciplined execution, continuous improvement, and strategic alignment within the organization. As we delve deeper into the roles and their responsibilities, it becomes evident how each contributes to unlocking the full potential of the OKR framework and driving organizational success

CHAPTER ELEVEN

Points to Consider before setting up OKRs

Setting up OKRs (Objectives and Key Results) for any entity requires thorough consideration and strategic planning. Here are several key points to consider to ensure the OKRs are effective and aligned with the organization's overall goals and capabilities:

1. What are your goals, and how many do you have?

Clarity of Goals: Clearly define what you want to achieve. Goals should be specific, measurable, achievable, relevant, and time-bound (SMART).

Number of Goals: Avoid setting too many goals. Focus on a few high-impact objectives to maintain clarity and avoid spreading resources too thin.

2. Why did you choose these goals?

Alignment with Vision: Ensure that the chosen goals align with the organization's long-term vision and mission.

Strategic Importance: Prioritize goals based on their strategic importance and potential impact on the business.

Stakeholder Input: Consider input from key stakeholders to ensure the goals are relevant and have broad support.

3. Do you have the capabilities to reach your goals?

Resource Availability: Assess whether you have the necessary resources (financial, human, technological) to achieve your goals.

Skill Sets: Ensure your team has the required skills and competencies. Identify any skill gaps and plan for training or hiring if necessary.

Support Systems: Evaluate if you have the right processes, tools, and support systems in place to facilitate goal achievement.

4. How long will it take to reach them?

Timeframe: Set realistic timelines for achieving your goals. Consider the complexity of the objectives and the time required for implementation.

Milestones: Break down long-term goals into smaller milestones to track progress and maintain momentum.

5. What factors could inhibit reaching them?

Risks and Challenges: Identify potential obstacles and risks that could impede progress, such as market changes, competition, or internal issues.

Contingency Plans: Develop contingency plans to address these challenges and mitigate risks.

6. What factors could accelerate the process?

Enablers: Identify factors that could accelerate goal achievement, such as new technologies, partnerships, or favorable market conditions.

Leverage Strengths: Utilize your organization's strengths and core competencies to gain an advantage and speed up progress.

7. What data and evidence do you have that you can achieve your goals in this OKR cycle?

Historical Data: Analyze past performance data to set realistic and informed goals.

Market Research: Use market research and industry benchmarks to validate your objectives.

Feasibility Studies: Conduct feasibility studies to ensure that your goals are achievable within the given timeframe and resources.

8. Are the goals you are setting ambitious yet achievable?

Balanced Ambition: Set goals that are challenging enough to inspire and drive performance but also realistic enough to be achievable.

Stretch Goals: Incorporate stretch goals to push the organization to higher performance levels without setting up for failure.

<u>**Industry and Departments**</u>

Industry Variations: Different industries have unique characteristics, operations, and sales cycles, which influence goal-setting timelines and priorities.

Departmental Goals: Tailor goals to specific departments, recognizing that each department may have different functions, timelines, and metrics.

<u>**Company Size and Nature**</u>

Startups: Focus on rapid growth, market penetration, and product development. OKRs should be short-term and highly flexible.

Scale-ups: Emphasize scaling operations, improving efficiency, and expanding market reach. OKRs should balance short-term agility with longer-term strategic goals.

Enterprises: Concentrate on sustaining growth, innovation, and market leadership. OKRs should be more structured, with a mix of short-term and long-term objectives.

<u>**Macro Influences**</u>

Economic Factors: Consider the impact of economic conditions on your business. Plan for scenarios such as recessions or economic booms.

Geopolitical Factors: Assess potential geopolitical risks and their implications for your business operations and goal achievement.

Micro Influences

Competitive Landscape: Monitor competitive activities and disruptions that could affect your market position and strategy.

Supply Chain Risks: Evaluate and mitigate risks within your supply chain to ensure smooth operations.

Internal Issues: Address internal challenges, such as company culture, employee engagement, and alignment between strategy and execution. Strengthening these areas can significantly enhance the likelihood of achieving your goals.

Conclusion

Setting up OKRs requires careful consideration of various factors to ensure they are meaningful, achievable, and aligned with the organization's strategic direction. By thoroughly evaluating your goals, capabilities, timelines, and potential risks and opportunities, you can create a robust OKR framework that drives performance and fosters organizational growth. Regularly reviewing and adjusting your OKRs based on feedback and changing circumstances will help maintain their relevance and effectiveness.

CHAPTER TWELVE

Chapter: OKRs Framework, Do's and Dont's of OKRs

The OKR (Objectives and Key Results) framework is designed to help organizations align and achieve their strategic objectives, guiding them from purpose to the ultimate vision through a holistic approach. Here's how it enables this journey through a 360-degree discipline approach:

<u>Clarity of Purpose and Vision:</u>

Purpose: OKRs start with a clear understanding of the organization's purpose. This is the 'why' behind what the organization does, providing meaning and direction to its activities.

Vision: The vision represents the ultimate long-term goal or destination that the organization aspires to achieve. It defines what success looks like in the future.

<u>Alignment of Objectives:</u>

OKRs help align individual and team objectives with the organization's overall purpose and vision. Each objective set within the framework should contribute directly to advancing the organization towards its vision.

This alignment ensures that everyone in the organization understands how their work contributes to the larger goals, fostering a sense of purpose and cohesion.

Discipline in Execution:

OKRs encourage disciplined execution by setting clear and measurable objectives (Objectives) and outcomes (Key Results).

Key Results are specific, quantifiable metrics that define the success criteria for achieving each Objective. This clarity helps teams stay focused and prioritize efforts effectively.

Continuous Improvement and Learning:

The 360-degree discipline approach involves continuous feedback and learning. Regular check-ins and reviews of OKRs allow teams to assess progress, identify challenges, and make necessary adjustments.

This iterative process promotes agility and responsiveness, ensuring that the organization can adapt to changes in the market or internal environment.

Cascading Alignment:

OKRs are typically cascaded throughout the organization, from top-level strategic objectives down to individual team or departmental goals.

This cascading ensures that every level of the organization is aligned towards achieving the overarching vision, creating a unified effort towards success.

Culture of Accountability and Transparency:

OKRs promote a culture of accountability by making objectives and results visible to everyone in the organization.

Transparency in goal-setting and progress tracking fosters trust and encourages collaboration across teams, enhancing overall organizational effectiveness.

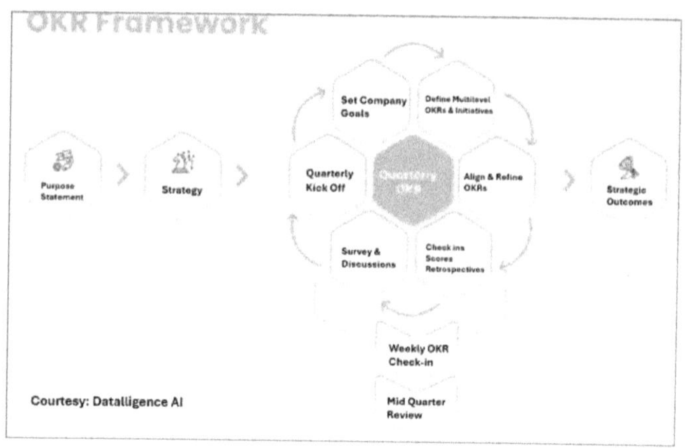

OKR Framework: Achieving Execution Excellence through disciplined approach

OKRs Framework Explained

The OKRs (Objectives and Key Results) framework is a powerful tool for setting and achieving goals in organizations. It consists of two main components:

Objectives: The "Whats"

Objectives define the overarching goals and intentions of the organization, teams, or individuals within the OKR framework. They:

Express goals and intentions clearly.

Are ambitious yet achievable, pushing teams to strive for excellence.

Should be tangible and straightforward, leaving no room for ambiguity.

Provide significant value upon successful achievement, contributing directly to the organization's strategic priorities.

Key Results: The "Hows"

Key Results outline the measurable milestones that indicate progress towards achieving the Objectives and define what success looks like. They:

Express specific outcomes that signify achievement, rather than merely describing activities.

Must be measurable, allowing for clear assessment of progress and success.

Include credible evidence of completion, ensuring accountability and transparency in the OKR process.

By defining clear Objectives (the "Whats") and measurable Key Results (the "Hows"), organizations can effectively implement the OKR framework to drive focused action, monitor progress, and achieve meaningful results aligned with their strategic goals. This structured approach ensures that OKRs serve as a powerful tool for performance management and continuous improvement within the organization.

Steps of OKR Framework

1. **Choosing the Right Timing for OKRs:** Setting OKRs at the appropriate intervals (e.g., quarterly or annually) ensures alignment with strategic planning cycles and allows for timely adjustments based on business dynamics.

2. **Ensuring Alignment of Goals Across the Organization:** Aligning employee objectives with organizational goals fosters unity of purpose and ensures that everyone is contributing towards achieving strategic outcomes.

3. **Defining Clear Objectives at Every Level:** Setting departmental and individual OKRs that are specific, measurable, and aligned with higher-level objectives ensures clarity in priorities and promotes focused efforts

towards shared goals.

4. Linking OKRs to Recognition and Motivation: Connecting OKR achievements with rewards and incentives motivates employees to strive for excellence, enhances accountability, and reinforces desired behaviors aligned with organizational success.

5. Embedding OKRs into Organizational DNA: Making OKRs an integral part of company culture involves promoting transparency, fostering a growth mindset, and cultivating a continuous improvement ethos through regular OKR reviews, feedback loops, and learning from both successes and challenges.

These steps collectively form a structured approach to implementing OKRs effectively within an organization, driving alignment, motivation, and sustained performance towards strategic objectives.

<u>Do's of OKRs:</u>

Emphasize the Why: Aligning OKRs with the organization's values and purpose helps foster buy-in and commitment from stakeholders. It ensures that every Objective contributes meaningfully to the organization's mission, keeping teams motivated and focused.

Establish a Cadence of Communication: Regular discussions about OKRs ensure alignment across the organization. This includes sharing progress, clarifying goals, and discussing next steps. Transparency in communication fosters accountability and collective effort towards achieving Objectives.

Keep OKRs Flexible: Flexibility allows teams to adapt to changing circumstances without losing sight of their goals. It encourages innovation and responsiveness to market shifts or customer needs, ensuring that OKRs remain relevant and impactful throughout their lifecycle.

Get Buy-in of Participants: Addressing the key questions of what, why, and how regarding OKRs is crucial for gaining buy-in:

What are we going to do? Define the Objectives clearly.

Why are we doing it? Connect Objectives to the organization's purpose and strategy.

What is in it for me? Explain how achieving the OKRs benefits individuals and teams.

How do we do it? Outline the strategies and actions needed to achieve the Objectives.

How do we do it well? Provide guidance on best practices and resources.

How can we make sure OKRs stick? Encourage commitment and continuous improvement in OKR implementation.

<u>The Don'ts ...</u>.

Failing to Differentiate Between Committed and Aspirational OKRs: It's important to distinguish between OKRs that teams are expected to achieve (committed) and those that stretch their capabilities (aspirational). This balance ensures both accountability and ambition.

Writing OKRs Based Solely on Belief Systems: OKRs should be informed by market conditions, customer feedback, and other external factors. Failing to update OKRs based on these inputs can lead to irrelevance or missed opportunities.

Setting Too Low OKRs: Objectives that are easily achievable without stretching teams can indicate underutilization of resources and missed potential for growth. OKRs should challenge teams to perform at their best while remaining achievable with concerted effort.

Insufficient Key Results: Key Results should be specific, measurable, and actionable. Setting vague or inadequate Key Results makes it difficult for teams to track progress effectively and achieve their Objectives.

By adhering to these principles and avoiding common pitfalls, organizations can effectively implement OKRs to drive performance, foster innovation, and achieve strategic objectives with clarity and focus.

By leveraging the OKR framework in a 360-degree disciplined approach, organizations can effectively translate their purpose into actionable objectives, align efforts across all levels, and systematically progress towards realizing their long-term vision. This structured approach not only enhances strategic focus but also promotes organizational agility and resilience in a dynamic business environment.

CHAPTER THIRTEEN

OKR Implementation - Preparation

Understanding Organizational Readiness:

Explanation: Assess the organization's current state and readiness for OKRs implementation. This includes evaluating culture, leadership buy-in, and existing performance management practices.

Example: Conduct stakeholder interviews and surveys to gauge perceptions and readiness levels. Assess if there is alignment between leadership vision and employee expectations.

Consequence of Not Following: Without assessing readiness, there may be resistance from employees or misalignment with organizational goals, leading to poor adoption and implementation challenges.

2. Setting Clear Objectives and Expectations:

Explanation: Define clear objectives and articulate the expected outcomes of implementing OKRs. Align OKRs with the organization's strategic priorities and communicate the benefits to stakeholders.

Example: Clearly communicate that the objective is to improve customer satisfaction by 15% and explain how OKRs will help achieve this through specific initiatives like launching a customer feedback portal.

Consequence of Not Following: Without setting clear objectives and expectations, there may be confusion among teams about the purpose of OKRs, resulting in misalignment and lack of focus on strategic priorities.

3. Establishing OKR Framework and Guidelines:

Explanation: Develop a framework that outlines how OKRs will be structured, managed, and evaluated. Define guidelines for setting SMART (Specific, Measurable, Achievable, Relevant, Time-bound) objectives and key results.

Example: Establish criteria for setting OKRs, such as limiting to 3 Objectives and 4 Key Results per Objective, to ensure focus and clarity.

Consequence of Not Following: Without a clear framework and guidelines, OKRs may lack specificity and measurability, making it challenging to track progress and assess achievement effectively.

4. Training and Capacity Building:

Explanation: Provide training and workshops to educate employees on OKR principles, methodology, and benefits. Build capabilities within teams to set, manage, and achieve OKRs effectively.

Example: Conduct workshops on setting effective OKRs, using OKR software tools, and conducting progress reviews to empower teams.

Consequence of Not Following: Insufficient training may lead to confusion or improper implementation of OKRs, reducing their effectiveness and limiting their impact on organizational performance.

5. Selecting OKR Software and Tools:

Explanation: Evaluate and choose appropriate OKR software or tools that align with organizational needs and facilitate OKR management, tracking, and transparency.

Example: Implement software that allows real-time tracking of OKR progress, collaboration across teams, and visualization of key metrics.

Consequence of Not Following: Using inadequate or outdated tools may hinder communication, transparency, and efficiency in OKR management, impacting overall implementation and adoption.

6. Pilot Testing and Iteration:

Explanation: Conduct pilot tests with a select group of teams to refine OKR processes, identify challenges, and gather feedback before full-scale implementation.

Example: Pilot test OKRs with one department to assess feasibility, refine Key Results, and adjust the framework based on initial results and feedback.

Consequence of Not Following: Skipping pilot testing may result in unforeseen challenges during full implementation, such as unrealistic objectives or inadequate alignment with team capabilities.

7. Establishing Communication Channels:

Explanation: Set up regular communication channels to keep stakeholders informed about OKR progress, updates, and successes. Foster transparency and alignment throughout the organization.

Example: Hold monthly town hall meetings to discuss OKR achievements, challenges, and adjustments with all employees.

Consequence of Not Following: Poor communication can lead to misinformation, lack of clarity, and reduced engagement with OKRs, undermining their effectiveness and organizational alignment.

8. Defining Success Metrics and Evaluation Criteria:

Explanation: Establish metrics to measure OKR success, such as alignment with strategic goals, achievement rates, and employee engagement levels. Define evaluation criteria to assess impact.

Example: Measure success by achieving a 90% completion rate on Key Results within the set timeframe.

Consequence of Not Following: Without clear success metrics and evaluation criteria, it becomes difficult to gauge the impact of OKRs on organizational performance and alignment with strategic objectives.

9. Creating a Change Management Plan:

Explanation: Develop a change management plan to address resistance, promote adoption, and foster a culture of continuous improvement with OKRs.

Example: Conduct change management workshops to prepare employees for the transition to OKRs, addressing concerns and emphasizing benefits.

Consequence of Not Following: Inadequate change management can result in resistance to OKRs, lack of buy-in from employees, and challenges in integrating OKRs into daily operations effectively.

10. Aligning OKRs with Performance Management:

Explanation: Integrate OKRs into existing performance management processes, ensuring alignment with individual and team goals, development plans, and career progression. However there are different schools of thought that voice against this as the tendency to maximise performance for assessment may hinder the setting up of aspirational & stretch goals. This has to be done with caution on a case to case basis.

Example: Link OKR achievements to performance reviews in a small way and recognition programs to reinforce alignment with organizational goals.

Consequence of Not Following: Without alignment with performance management, OKRs may be perceived as separate from daily responsibilities, leading to disengagement and reduced accountability.

11. Anticipating Challenges and Mitigation Strategies:

Explanation: Identify potential challenges to OKR implementation, such as resource constraints or cultural barriers. Develop proactive strategies to mitigate risks and adapt OKR processes.

Example: Allocate additional resources for teams facing capacity constraints to ensure they can effectively pursue their OKRs.

Consequence of Not Following: Failing to anticipate challenges may result in delays, setbacks, or failure to achieve OKRs, impacting organizational performance and employee morale.

12. Establishing a Timeline and Milestones:

Explanation: Create a timeline with clear milestones and deadlines for each phase of OKR implementation, from preparation and rollout to ongoing management and review.

Example: Set a timeline for completing training sessions, conducting pilot tests, and launching full-scale OKR implementation within six months.

Consequence of Not Following: Without a timeline, OKR implementation may lack structure and accountability, leading to delays or incomplete adoption across the organization.

Summary

Preparing for OKRs is critical for laying the groundwork for successful implementation and maximizing their impact on organizational performance. Each step in this chapter ensures alignment, clarity, and readiness across the organization, fostering a culture of accountability and continuous improvement with OKRs. By following these preparatory steps and examples, organizations can enhance their ability to set, manage, and achieve strategic objectives effectively through OKRs.

OKR Implementation: Crafting effective OKRs

Implementing OKRs begins with crafting effective OKRs (Objectives and Key Results) that align with organizational goals and drive performance. This step involves defining clear and actionable objectives, along with measurable key results that indicate progress towards those objectives.

Sample OKR Template

Objectives set the direction, but key results drive progress toward achieving those objectives. Many companies make the mistake of only defining objectives, but it's the key results that truly set you apart. Consider this: your competitors likely have similar objectives, but what distinguishes your company is the ability to think through, define, achieve, and adjust those key results. Key results are the real differentiators that turn goals into measurable success.

<u>**Here's how to craft effective OKRs:**</u>

Crafting Effective Company Objectives: A Strategic Blueprint

Defining Strategic Priorities for Success

Companies often label their key goals as strategic priorities, objectives, areas of focus, or themes. The terminology varies, but the purpose is the same: to establish 3 to 5 clear objectives that guide the entire organization towards desired outcomes over the next 1 to 3 years. To effectively draft these objectives, companies should consider the following:

Core Purpose: Define the fundamental reason for your company's existence. This purpose should emotionally connect your team to the company's mission beyond profit-making. For example, qilo aims to help CEOs accelerate growth and empower employees to reach their full potential.

Uniqueness: Identify what makes your company and its products/services stand out from the competition.

Competitive Edge: Determine what your company does best in serving customers and identify any gaps hindering this potential.

Operational Efficiency: Address any gaps in effectively and efficiently delivering your products/services to customers.

Growth Barriers: Identify the top three obstacles to achieving higher sales and margin growth.

Future Goals: Outline what you want to achieve in the next 2 to 3 years.

Insights and Hypotheses: Specify the insights needed or hypotheses to validate for sustained cash flow and profitability.

General Guidelines for Crafting Objectives:

The CEO should define a "big-arrow" (a major sales target) and create a list of potential company objectives to achieve this target.

Ensure all objectives are mutually exclusive.

Prioritize and make trade-offs when drafting objectives.

Involve all functional heads in discussing and finalizing these objectives to ensure buy-in.

Common Mistakes to Avoid:

Avoid generic objectives that could apply to competitors.

Ensure objectives are clear and easy to understand.

Limit objectives to 3 or 4 key goals.

Do not define specific key results within these objectives.

Collaborate with the leadership team in brainstorming sessions to refine objectives.

Your big-arrow and company objectives set the strategic direction and leadership priorities for the next 12 months. All key performance indicators (KPIs) and action plans should align with and support these objectives.

OKR Implementation: Crafting Effective OKRs

1. Define Clear Objectives:

Explanation: Objectives in OKRs articulate what you want to achieve. They should be concise, inspiring, and directly linked to the organization's strategic priorities.

Example:

Objective: Increase customer satisfaction.

Explanation: This objective is clear and focuses on improving a specific aspect of business performance that aligns with overall goals.

2. Establish Measurable Key Results:

Explanation: Key Results (KRs) define measurable outcomes that indicate progress towards achieving the Objectives. They should be specific, measurable, achievable, relevant, and time-bound (SMART).

Example:

Key Result: Achieve a Net Promoter Score (NPS) of 80%.

Explanation: This Key Result provides a clear metric (NPS) and a specific target (80%), allowing teams to track progress and success.

3. Ensure Alignment and Ambition:

Explanation: OKRs should stretch teams to achieve ambitious goals while remaining achievable within the given timeframe. They should align with departmental and organizational priorities.

Example:

Objective: Launch a new product line.

Key Result: Achieve $1 million in revenue from the new product line by the end of the fiscal year.

Explanation: This OKR aligns with the strategic objective of expanding product offerings and sets an ambitious yet realistic revenue target.

4. Focus on Outcomes, Not Activities:

Explanation: Key Results should focus on outcomes and results, not on tasks or activities. They should reflect the impact and success of achieving the Objectives.

Example:

Objective: Improve operational efficiency.

Key Result: Reduce average production time by 20%.

Explanation: This Key Result measures the outcome (reduced production time) rather than the activities involved in achieving it.

5. Make OKRs Transparent and Accessible:

Explanation: OKRs should be transparent and accessible to all team members. Clear communication of OKRs ensures alignment, accountability, and shared understanding across the organization.

Example:

Share OKRs: Publish OKRs on a company-wide dashboard or intranet.

Explanation: This transparency fosters a culture of openness and collaboration, enabling teams to see how their objectives contribute to broader organizational goals.

6. Review and Refine Regularly:

Explanation: OKRs should be dynamic and adaptable to changing circumstances. Regularly review progress, reassess Key Results, and make adjustments as necessary to stay on track.

Example:

Review Cycle: Conduct quarterly OKR reviews.

Explanation: This periodic review allows teams to evaluate performance, celebrate successes, and realign priorities based on market conditions or organizational shifts.

Benefits of Crafting Effective OKRs

Crafting effective OKRs ensures clarity of purpose, alignment with strategic goals, and actionable metrics to track progress effectively. It encourages teams to focus on outcomes that drive organizational success while fostering a culture of accountability and continuous improvement.

Consequences of Ineffective OKRs

Lack of Clarity: Unclear Objectives and vague Key Results can lead to confusion among team members about priorities and expectations.

Misalignment: Objectives that do not align with organizational goals may result in wasted resources and efforts on irrelevant initiatives.

Lack of Motivation: If Key Results are not measurable or achievable, teams may feel demotivated or lose sight of the impact of their work.

Difficulty in Tracking Progress: Without measurable Key Results, it becomes challenging to assess progress towards achieving Objectives, making it difficult to course-correct or celebrate successes.

In summary, crafting effective OKRs involves setting clear, measurable objectives aligned with organizational priorities and defining actionable Key Results that drive performance and foster accountability across teams.

CHAPTER FIFTEEN

OKR implementation – Deploying OKRs across Organisation

Deploying OKRs across teams involves a structured approach to ensure alignment, engagement, and effective execution. This chapter provides a comprehensive guide on how to roll out OKRs at the team level, fostering a culture of transparency, collaboration, and continuous improvement.

Scaling Strategies for OKR Deployment

Scaling OKRs effectively requires choosing the right strategy to align with your organization's needs and culture. Here are different scaling strategies with explanations and examples:

1. Top-Down Scaling

Explanation: In top-down scaling, senior leadership defines the high-level organizational objectives and cascades them down to departments and teams. Each level then sets its own OKRs in alignment with these overarching goals.

Example:

Organizational Objective: Increase market share by 10%.

Marketing Department Objective: Enhance brand visibility.

Team Objective: Launch a social media campaign to increase engagement by 25%.

Advantages:

Ensures strong alignment with strategic goals.

Provides clear direction and priorities from leadership.

Disadvantages:

May limit team autonomy.

Risk of disconnect if not well-communicated.

2. Bottom-Up Scaling

Explanation: In bottom-up scaling, teams and departments set their own OKRs based on their understanding of what needs to be achieved. These OKRs are then reviewed and aligned with the organization's strategic goals by senior leadership.

Example:

Team Objective: Improve customer service response time by 20%.

Department Objective: Enhance overall customer satisfaction.

Advantages:

Encourages team ownership and engagement.

Utilizes frontline insights for realistic goal-setting.

Disadvantages:

Potential misalignment with strategic goals.

Requires strong communication and alignment mechanisms.

3. Mixed Scaling

Explanation: Mixed scaling combines elements of both top-down and bottom-up approaches. Leadership sets high-level strategic priorities, while teams develop OKRs that align with these priorities and address their unique challenges.

Example:

Organizational Objective: Achieve operational excellence.

Leadership Guidance: Focus on efficiency and quality.

Team Objective: Reduce production defects by 30%.

Advantages:

Balances strategic alignment with team autonomy.

Encourages both leadership direction and team innovation.

Disadvantages:

Can be complex to manage and coordinate.

Requires effective communication and collaboration.

Tips for Scaling OKRs

Scaling OKRs successfully involves turning employees and participants into ambassadors of the program. Here are tips to address concerns, overcome resistance, and make participants key proponents of the scale-up process:

1. Communicate the Vision and Benefits

Explanation: Clearly articulate the vision and benefits of OKRs to all employees. Explain how OKRs align with the organization's goals and how they can benefit individual and team performance.

Example: Host town hall meetings and workshops to discuss the strategic importance of OKRs and share success stories from pilot phases.

2. Involve Employees Early and Often

Explanation: Engage employees early in the OKR process. Involve them in setting their own OKRs to ensure buy-in and commitment.

Example: Form cross-functional OKR working groups to gather input and ideas from different teams.

3. Provide Adequate Training and Support

Explanation: Offer comprehensive training on OKR methodology, tools, and best practices. Ensure ongoing support through resources like FAQs, helpdesks, and coaching sessions.

Example: Conduct regular training sessions, create an OKR resource hub, and assign OKR coaches to assist teams.

4. Foster a Culture of Collaboration and Transparency

Explanation: Encourage open communication and collaboration across teams. Share OKRs publicly within the organization to foster transparency and alignment.

Example: Use OKR software to make OKRs visible to everyone, and schedule regular inter-team meetings to discuss progress and challenges.

5. Recognize and Reward Success

Explanation: Celebrate achievements and milestones. Recognize and reward individuals and teams who successfully meet their OKRs, reinforcing the value of their efforts.

Example: Implement a recognition program that highlights OKR accomplishments during company meetings and offers incentives like bonuses or awards.

6. Address Concerns and Overcome Resistance

Explanation: Be proactive in addressing concerns and resistance. Listen to employee feedback and make necessary adjustments to the OKR process.

Example: Conduct anonymous surveys to gather feedback on OKR implementation and hold feedback sessions to discuss and address common concerns.

7. Make OKRs Part of the Company Culture

Explanation: Integrate OKRs into the daily workflow and company culture. Reinforce the importance of OKRs through regular communication and by embedding them in performance reviews and planning processes.

Example: Include OKR discussions in team meetings, quarterly reviews, and annual performance appraisals.

Benefits of Following These Tips

Enhanced Engagement: Employees feel valued and engaged when they see the relevance and impact of OKRs on their work.

Improved Alignment: Clear communication and collaboration ensure that OKRs are aligned with organizational goals and team efforts.

Sustained Success: A supportive culture and recognition of achievements foster a sustainable OKR program that drives continuous improvement.

Consequences of Not Following These Tips

Low Buy-In: Without clear communication and involvement, employees may feel disconnected and unmotivated, leading to poor adoption of OKRs.

Misalignment: Lack of transparency and collaboration can result in misaligned objectives and inefficient use of resources.

Resistance to Change: Ignoring feedback and not addressing concerns can lead to resistance, hindering the success of the OKR program.

<u>Steps to Deploy OKRs Across Teams</u>

1. Aligning Team OKRs with Organizational Goals

Explanation: Ensure that each team's OKRs are aligned with the broader organizational objectives. This alignment helps to maintain a clear line of sight from individual contributions to overall strategic goals.

Example: If the company's objective is to increase market share by 10%, the marketing team might have an objective to "Enhance brand visibility," with key results such as "Increase social media engagement by 25%" and "Launch three major PR campaigns."

Consequence of Not Following: Misalignment can lead to wasted efforts on irrelevant activities, reducing overall impact and causing confusion about priorities.

2. Conducting OKR Workshops and Training

Explanation: Organize workshops and training sessions to educate teams on how to set effective OKRs. This includes understanding the OKR framework, setting ambitious yet achievable goals, and defining measurable key results.

Example: Conduct a workshop where team leaders and members learn to craft OKRs. Provide templates and examples, and allow teams to practice setting their own OKRs.

Consequence of Not Following: Without proper training, teams may struggle to set meaningful OKRs, leading to poorly defined objectives and key results that are hard to measure and achieve.

3. Encouraging Team Collaboration

Explanation: Promote collaboration within and between teams to ensure cohesive OKR setting and execution. Encourage teams to discuss their OKRs, share insights, and align their efforts.

Example: Schedule cross-functional meetings where teams share their OKRs and identify opportunities for collaboration. For instance, the sales team might coordinate with the product team to align on product launch timelines and sales targets.

Consequence of Not Following: Lack of collaboration can result in silos, duplicated efforts, and missed opportunities for synergy, ultimately hampering overall performance.

4. Setting Up Regular Check-ins and Reviews

Explanation: Establish a cadence of regular check-ins and reviews to monitor progress, address challenges, and make necessary adjustments. This keeps OKRs dynamic and responsive to changing circumstances.

Example: Hold bi-weekly check-in meetings where teams review their progress on OKRs, discuss roadblocks, and update their key results as needed.

Consequence of Not Following: Irregular or infrequent check-ins can lead to a loss of focus, unaddressed obstacles, and failure to achieve objectives due to a lack of timely interventions.

5. Using OKR Software and Tools

Explanation: Implement OKR software and tools to facilitate tracking, transparency, and collaboration. These tools help in managing OKRs efficiently and provide real-time visibility into progress.

Example: Use an OKR management platform where teams can input their OKRs, update progress, and visualize alignment with organizational goals through dashboards and reports.

Consequence of Not Following: Relying on manual processes or inadequate tools can lead to inefficiencies, lack of visibility, and difficulty in tracking progress and outcomes accurately.

6. Fostering a Culture of Accountability

Explanation: Encourage a culture of accountability where teams take ownership of their OKRs. This involves recognizing achievements, learning from failures, and continuously striving for improvement.

Example: Celebrate team successes when OKRs are achieved and conduct retrospectives to learn from any missed targets. Use these insights to improve future OKR setting and execution.

Consequence of Not Following: Without a culture of accountability, teams may lack the motivation and commitment to achieve their OKRs, leading to subpar performance and disengagement.

7. Gathering Feedback and Iterating

Explanation: Continuously gather feedback from teams on the OKR process and make iterative improvements. This ensures that the OKR framework evolves to meet the organization's needs effectively.

Example: After each OKR cycle, collect feedback through surveys and focus groups. Use this input to refine OKR guidelines, training programs, and tools.

Consequence of Not Following: Ignoring feedback can result in persistent issues and declining engagement with OKRs, reducing their effectiveness and potential benefits.

Summary

Deploying OKRs across teams requires careful planning, effective communication, and ongoing support. By choosing the right scaling strategy and following best practices for engagement and alignment, organizations can turn employees into ambassadors of the OKR program, ensuring its success and driving overall performance. Through a combination of top-down, bottom-up, or mixed scaling approaches, and by implementing tips to address concerns and foster a culture of accountability, teams can effectively set and achieve their OKRs, contributing to the broader organizational objectives and continuous improvement.

CHAPTER SIXTEEN

OKR Implementation Challenges & Best Practices

Implementing OKRs effectively requires understanding their role, fostering team-based collaboration, maintaining regular reviews, and focusing on measurable results. Below are the best practices for successful OKR implementation, supplemented with examples, challenges, and consequences of not following each step.

Challenges in Implementing OKRs

Lack of Clarity: Unclear objectives and key results can lead to confusion and misalignment.

Resistance to Change: Employees may resist adopting OKRs due to unfamiliarity or perceived extra workload.

Overloading Objectives: Setting too many OKRs can overwhelm teams and dilute focus.

Inconsistent Scoring: Without a uniform scoring system, evaluating progress becomes challenging.

Infrequent Reviews: Not reviewing OKRs regularly can result in missed opportunities for course correction.

Poor Alignment: Misalignment between team and organizational OKRs can hinder overall success.

Lack of Ownership: Without designated ownership, accountability for OKRs can falter.

Best Practices for Overcoming Challenges

1. Understanding the Role of OKRs vs. Initiatives

Explanation: OKRs define what you want to achieve (Objectives) and how you measure success (Key Results), while initiatives are specific actions taken to achieve these goals. Differentiating them ensures clarity and focus.

Example:

Objective: Improve customer satisfaction.

Key Result: Increase customer satisfaction score from 70% to 85%.

Initiative: Launch a new customer feedback program.

Challenge: Confusion between OKRs and initiatives can dilute efforts. Consequence of Not Following: Blurring OKRs and initiatives can lead to confusion and diluted efforts, focusing on activities rather than outcomes.

2. Use Team-Based OKRs

Explanation: Setting OKRs at the team level promotes ownership and alignment with organizational goals, fostering collaboration.

Example: A product development team sets an OKR to "Reduce the average time to resolve bugs by 50%," aligning with the company's objective to improve product reliability.

Challenge: Lack of team collaboration and alignment. Consequence of Not Following: Without team-based OKRs, there may be a lack of alignment and motivation, as team members might not see how their work contributes to broader goals.

3. Implement a Weekly OKRs Progress Review

Explanation: Regular reviews help teams stay on track, identify obstacles early, and make necessary adjustments. These check-ins provide structured opportunities to assess progress.

Example: During weekly team meetings, members discuss their progress towards key results, such as "Achieve a 20% increase in user engagement by the end of the quarter," and address any roadblocks.

Challenge: Infrequent reviews leading to lost focus. Consequence of Not Following: Infrequent reviews can result in teams losing focus and failing to address issues promptly, reducing the likelihood of achieving their OKRs.

4. Don't Capture Business-as-Usual in Your OKRs

Explanation: OKRs should focus on breakthrough achievements and significant improvements, not routine tasks. This encourages teams to stretch beyond their comfort zones and drive innovation.

Example: Instead of setting an OKR to "Maintain current customer service response times," set an OKR to "Reduce average response time from 24 hours to 12 hours."

Challenge: Focusing on routine tasks rather than significant improvements. Consequence of Not Following: Including routine tasks in OKRs can lead to complacency and a lack of meaningful progress, focusing on maintaining the status quo rather than striving for excellence.

5. Limit Your OKRs to 3 Objectives and 4 KRs per Objective per Plan

Explanation: Keeping OKRs concise ensures focus and manageability. Limiting the number of objectives and key results prevents teams from being overwhelmed and allows better prioritization.

Example: A sales team might set the following OKRs for a quarter:

Objective 1: Increase quarterly sales revenue.

KR 1: Achieve $1 million in sales.

KR 2: Acquire 50 new customers.

KR 3: Increase the average deal size by 10%.

Challenge: Overloading teams with too many objectives. Consequence of Not Following: Setting too many OKRs can dilute focus and make it challenging to track and achieve goals effectively.

6. Distribute Ownership

Explanation: Assigning ownership of OKRs to specific team members ensures accountability and clarity on who is responsible for driving progress. Ownership fosters commitment and proactive management of key results.

Example: In a marketing team, one member could own the KR "Increase website traffic by 30%," while another owns "Generate 500 new leads."

Challenge: Lack of clear ownership and accountability. Consequence of Not Following: Without clear ownership, there might be ambiguity and lack of accountability, leading to poor follow-through on OKRs.

7. Avoid Individual OKRs

Explanation: Focusing on team OKRs promotes collaboration and alignment. Team OKRs ensure that all members work together towards shared goals.

Example: Instead of individual OKRs for each salesperson, set a team OKR like "Increase total team sales by 25%."

Challenge: Siloed efforts and lack of team cohesion. Consequence of Not Following: Individual OKRs can lead to siloed efforts and reduce overall cohesion and collaborative spirit within the team.

8. Measurable vs. Non-Measurable Key Results

Explanation: Key Results should be specific and measurable to track progress effectively. Measurable KRs provide clear criteria for success, while non-measurable KRs can lead to subjective interpretations.

Example:

Measurable KR: "Increase customer retention rate from 80% to 90%."

Non-Measurable KR: "Improve customer satisfaction."

Challenge: Ambiguity in tracking progress. Consequence of Not Following: Non-measurable KRs can lead to ambiguity and make it difficult to assess whether the objectives have been achieved.

9. OKRs Don't Cascade (But They Can Align)

Explanation: Instead of rigidly cascading OKRs from top to bottom, align them to ensure that each team's OKRs support broader organizational goals. This flexible approach fosters better alignment and adaptability.

Example: While the company's objective is to "Expand market presence," the sales team might set an aligned OKR to "Enter two new markets by the end of the year."

Challenge: Inflexibility and misalignment. Consequence of Not Following: Strict cascading can lead to inflexibility and misalignment, as lower-level OKRs might not fully reflect the realities and priorities of individual teams.

10. Write Meaningful Check-Ins

Explanation: Regular check-ins should be substantive and provide valuable insights into progress, challenges, and next steps. Meaningful check-ins help maintain momentum and address issues promptly.

Example: During a check-in, a team member reports, "We've achieved 50% of our target for increasing webinar attendance, but we need to increase promotional efforts to reach the remaining 50%."

Challenge: Superficial and ineffective check-ins. Consequence of Not Following: Superficial check-ins can lead to unresolved issues and lack of actionable insights, hindering progress.

11. Keep Scoring Consistent with the Rest of Your Organization

Explanation: Use a consistent scoring system across the organization to evaluate OKRs. This uniformity helps in comparing performance and understanding progress objectively.

Example: A common scoring system might be:

0.0-0.3: No progress.

0.4-0.6: Some progress, but not on track.

0.7-1.0: On track or achieved.

Challenge: Inconsistent progress evaluation. Consequence of Not Following: Inconsistent scoring can lead to confusion and misinterpretation of progress, making it difficult to assess overall performance accurately.

12. No More than 2 Yellow Statuses in a Row

Explanation: Track the status of OKRs regularly and ensure no objective stays in a cautionary (yellow) status for more than two consecutive review periods. Address issues proactively to avoid slipping into red status.

Example: If a Key Result is in yellow status for two weeks, the team should take corrective action to improve progress and move it back to green.

Challenge: Prolonged cautionary status without action. Consequence of Not Following: Allowing prolonged yellow statuses can lead to missed objectives and unaddressed risks, ultimately impacting the achievement of goals.

13. Keep Track of Your Initiatives and Action Items

Explanation: Regularly monitor initiatives and action items that support OKRs. Ensure they are progressing as planned and making the desired impact.

Example: For an OKR to "Increase product adoption by 20%," track related initiatives like "Conducting product webinars" and "Launching a customer onboarding program."

Challenge: Neglecting to track supporting actions. Consequence of Not Following: Neglecting to track initiatives can result in delayed actions and ineffective execution, jeopardizing the achievement of OKRs.

14. Monthly Confidence Health Check on Objectives

Explanation: Perform monthly health checks to gauge confidence levels in achieving OKRs. Use these checks to make necessary adjustments and keep teams on track.

Example: During a monthly review, a team might reassess their confidence in achieving the KR "Increase monthly active users by 15%" and identify additional marketing efforts needed to boost user acquisition.

Challenge: Missing early warning signs. Consequence of Not Following: Without regular health checks, teams might miss early warning signs of issues, leading to unmet objectives and lower performance.

15. Make Trends Easy to See

Explanation: Use visual tools and dashboards to make trends in OKR progress easily visible. This transparency helps teams quickly understand

their status and take corrective actions.

Example: An OKR dashboard showing progress bars and trend lines for each KR, highlighting areas that are ahead or behind schedule.

Challenge: Lack of visibility into progress trends. Consequence of Not Following: Lack of visibility into trends can make it difficult for teams to understand their progress and respond effectively, potentially leading to missed deadlines and objectives.

Conclusion

Implementing OKRs effectively requires adherence to best practices that foster alignment, engagement, and continuous improvement. By differentiating OKRs from initiatives, leveraging team-based OKRs, maintaining regular reviews, and focusing on measurable results, organizations can drive significant progress towards their strategic goals. Addressing challenges such as lack of clarity, resistance to change, and inconsistent scoring ensures that OKRs are not just set but are actively managed and achieved, leading to meaningful organizational growth and success.

CHAPTER SEVENTEEN

OKR Ceremonies

Effective management of OKRs throughout their lifecycle is crucial for ensuring alignment, tracking progress, and achieving desired outcomes. This chapter details the key ceremonies and activities involved in managing OKRs, from setting objectives to regular check-ins, evaluation, and retrospectives.

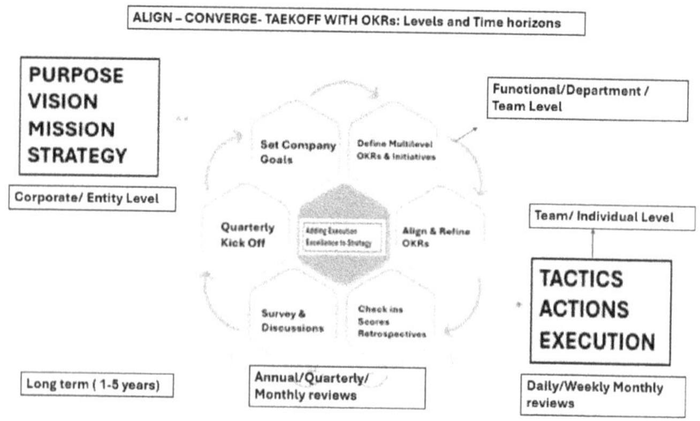

OKR review timelines & Ceremonies at different levels

Integrating Review Routines with OKRs for Success

Regular, periodic review through pre-scheduled cadences and checkins are crucial for driving execution and maintaining focus. Many teams and managers enthusiastically set their OKRs, but often lose focus once they return to their day-to-day tasks. This happens because daily tasks often seem more urgent, while OKRs are important but less urgent. To keep the focus on OKRs and ensure their successful execution, regular review sessions are essential.

Importance of OKR Review Sessions

OKR review sessions help maintain the focus on achieving key results and ensure that objectives remain a priority despite daily urgencies. These sessions should be conducted weekly, bi-weekly, or monthly, depending on the team's preference, to keep the momentum going. The primary agenda of these sessions is to refocus efforts on key results, update progress, and make necessary adjustments.

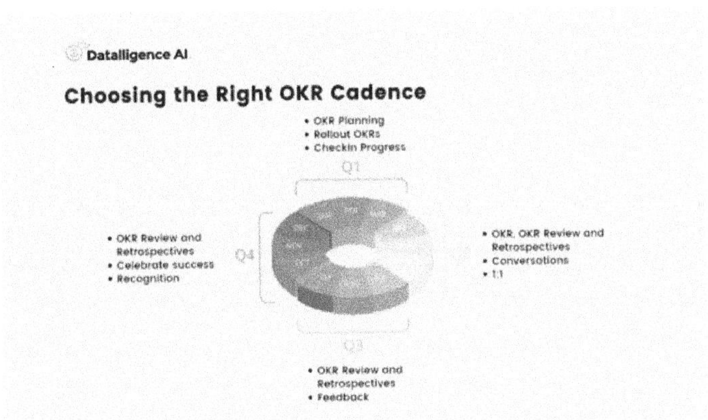

Different Cadences with different agendas

Steps to Conduct Effective OKR Review Sessions

Schedule the Session: The manager should set a date and time for the OKR review session. For a team of 4 to 6 members, this typically takes 90 to 120 minutes. For larger teams, divide them into smaller groups and conduct separate reviews.

Review Progress:

- Assess key results achieved by each team member.
- Identify challenges faced in achieving these key results.
- Provide Feedback and Adjust: The manager should give feedback, recognize achievements, and adjust key results as needed based on the current circumstances.

Checklists for Review Sessions

For Team Members:

Update progress on outcome-based key results.

Update progress on effort-based key results.

List the top three challenges faced in achieving the desired results.

For Managers:

Schedule the session and book necessary resources at least a week in advance.

Review key results due for completion by team members.

During the session, ensure each team member gets 10 to 15 minutes.

Provide quick feedback and recognize achievements.

After the session, acknowledge high performers via email or the company's recognition platform.

If it's the last month of the quarter, close the current OKRs and set new ones for the next quarter.

Common Mistakes to Avoid

Inconsistent Review Sessions: Ensure reviews are conducted on time, even if the manager is on leave. Appoint someone else to lead the session if needed.

Lack of Action on Review Outcomes: Act on the action items generated during the review to achieve key results.

Prolonged Sessions: Keep sessions brief and focused, avoiding other unrelated agendas.

Manager-Dominated Sessions: Allow team members to present their progress, fostering accountability.

Failure to Adjust Key Results: Regularly optimize key results. If they are too easy or too difficult, adjust them accordingly.The different types of meetings, ceremonies and cadencies undertaken through the OKR implementaiton cycle can be summarised as follows:

1. Kick Starter : Setting Objectives

Purpose: Set OKRs for the upcoming cycle.

Frequency: Yearly and quarterly.

Process:

The team answers the following questions:

What corporate OKRs can our team influence in this cycle?

What team OKRs can our team influence in this cycle? (e.g., what annual objectives will we influence in Q3?)

Are there additional local OKRs that are important? What are they?

Are there expectations and dependencies from other teams? What are they?

Contributors: All team members.

Value: This ceremony ensures the team focuses on strategy, creates links, and establishes cross-OKRs. It helps in aligning team efforts with corporate goals and identifying interdependencies and potential overlaps.

Example: A marketing team sets a quarterly OKR to "Increase social media engagement by 25%," aligning it with the corporate objective to "Boost brand visibility." They identify dependencies on the content team for new materials and the IT team for analytics support.

What Could Happen If Not Followed: Without a structured setting of objectives, teams may work in silos, leading to misalignment with corporate goals and inefficiencies due to unrecognized dependencies and overlaps.

2.Share the Progess: Regular Check-Ins (Interim Checkpoint)

Purpose: Team synchronization and timely response to deviations.

Frequency: Weekly, with an interim checkpoint in the middle of the cycle (quarter/year).

Process:

During the team meeting (stand-up, weekly), review current OKR scores and answer three questions:

Has the OKR score changed since last week?

Are we moving toward our OKRs at an adequate pace, and how likely are we to deliver our Key Results?

What prevents us from achieving our OKRs and how can we overcome these issues?

Contributors: All team members.

Value: Regular check-ins improve the manageability and predictability of team results by ensuring timely adjustments and keeping the team focused on their OKRs.

Example: A development team meets weekly to track progress on their objective to "Launch a new product feature," discussing blockers such as technical challenges and reallocating resources as needed to stay on track.

What Could Happen If Not Followed: Without regular check-ins, teams may not notice when they're off-track until it's too late to course-correct, leading to missed objectives and lower performance.

3. Take stock: Evaluation

Purpose: Wrap up the results of the cycle and determine progress towards OKRs.

Frequency: End of each cycle (year, quarter, month). Preliminary results should be summed up monthly, including annual and quarterly OKRs.

Process: Grade each KR and provide context/comments if necessary.

Contributors: All team members.

Value: Evaluating the results at the end of each cycle provides transparency and insights into the team's performance, helping to understand achievements and areas for improvement.

Example: At the end of Q2, the sales team evaluates their KR "Increase quarterly sales by 15%" and notes they achieved a 12% increase. They document reasons for falling short, such as market conditions and competition.

What Could Happen If Not Followed: Without proper evaluation, teams miss the opportunity to understand their performance comprehensively, leading to repeated mistakes and overlooked successes.

4. Retrospective : Reflect on the journey and plan for the next cycle

Purpose: Reflect on the results of the cycle and create a plan for improvement.

Frequency: Once a quarter and when complex issues arise, even between teams.

Process: Reflect on three components:

What went well?

What could be improved?

What 2-3 improvements will we implement over the next cycle?

Contributors: All team members.

Value: Continuous improvement of processes, quality, and results by learning from past experiences and planning actionable improvements.

Example: After a quarterly cycle, the customer service team holds a retrospective. They celebrate improved response times but note that training on new systems could be better. They plan to implement a more comprehensive training program for the next cycle.

What Could Happen If Not Followed: Skipping retrospectives can result in recurring issues and stagnation in processes and team development, as there is no formal mechanism for reflecting and improving.

Key Activities

1. Presenting OKRs to the Team:

Explanation: Share OKRs with the entire team to check for overlaps, dependencies, suggestions for improvement, and consistency with corporate goals.

Example: The project manager presents the team's OKRs during a team meeting, inviting feedback and ensuring everyone understands their role in achieving these goals.

Consequence of Not Following: Lack of clarity and misalignment, leading to duplicated efforts and missed dependencies.

2. Regular Review and Feedback:

Explanation: Regularly review progress and provide feedback to keep everyone aligned and motivated.

Example: A weekly review meeting where team members discuss their progress on OKRs and receive constructive feedback.

Consequence of Not Following: Teams may drift off course without timely feedback, reducing the likelihood of achieving their OKRs.

3. Celebrating Successes:

Explanation: Recognize and celebrate achievements to motivate and engage the team.

Example: Hosting a small celebration for the team when they meet a significant OKR milestone, such as completing a major project ahead of schedule.

Consequence of Not Following: Teams may feel unappreciated and demotivated, impacting future performance and morale.

<u>Enhancing Managerial Effectiveness</u>

For successful OKR implementation, managerial effectiveness is paramount. Managers must be able to answer key questions about their team's purpose, priorities, and impact on the business. Enhancing managerial capability will foster a culture of discipline, accountability, and high performance.

Steps to Enhance Managerial Effectiveness

Identify Great Managers: Understand what makes a great manager in the context of your business and culture.

Provide Training: Offer training that helps managers become better coaches.

Measure and Feedback: Regularly measure managerial effectiveness and provide constructive feedback.

By marrying your review routines with OKRs, ensuring consistent managerial buy-in, and maintaining a high level of effectiveness, organizations can achieve their strategic objectives and foster a culture of continuous improvement and accountability.

In summary, managing OKRs through the cycle involves a series of structured ceremonies and key activities to ensure alignment, track progress, and foster continuous improvement. By setting clear objectives, regularly checking in on progress, evaluating outcomes, and reflecting on learnings, teams can stay focused, motivated, and aligned with organizational goals. Additionally, involving the team in presenting OKRs, providing regular feedback, and celebrating successes helps to build a strong, collaborative, and motivated team culture.

CHAPTER EIGHTEEN

Measuring Success for CEOs

As a CEO, the ability to measure success effectively is crucial for steering your organization toward its strategic goals. OKRs (Objectives and Key Results) provide a powerful framework for setting, tracking, and achieving these goals. By implementing OKRs with urgency and dedication, you can harness the full energy of your employees, much like a magnifying glass focuses the sun's rays to ignite a fire. This chapter will delve into the intricacies of measuring success with OKRs, ensuring your organization achieves its objectives with precision and purpose.

The Importance of Measuring Success with OKRs

OKRs offer a clear, structured approach to goal-setting that aligns individual efforts with organizational objectives. Measuring success with OKRs is not just about tracking progress but also about driving accountability, transparency, and continuous improvement. Here are some key reasons why measuring success with OKRs is vital:

Alignment with Strategic Goals:

OKRs ensure that every team and individual is working towards the same strategic objectives, creating a cohesive and focused effort across the organization.

Example: A company with a strategic goal of becoming the market leader in customer satisfaction might set OKRs across all departments to enhance customer experience, streamline processes, and innovate product features.

Accountability and Ownership:

By clearly defining what needs to be achieved and how it will be measured, OKRs foster a culture of accountability and ownership.

Example: When a marketing team sets an OKR to "Increase website traffic by 20%," each member knows their role and contributions, driving a sense of responsibility and commitment.

Transparency and Communication:

OKRs provide a transparent framework that enhances communication and collaboration within and across teams.

Example: Regular OKR check-ins and updates ensure that everyone is aware of progress, challenges, and adjustments, fostering a collaborative environment.

Continuous Improvement:

The iterative nature of OKRs promotes a culture of continuous improvement, with regular reviews and reflections driving better performance.

Example: After completing an OKR cycle, teams reflect on what worked well and what didn't, using these insights to set more effective OKRs in the next cycle.

Setting Clear, Measurable OKRs

The foundation of measuring success with OKRs lies in setting clear, measurable objectives and key results. Here's how to ensure your OKRs are well-defined:

Specific and Clear Objectives:

Objectives should be specific, clear, and aligned with the strategic goals of the organization.

Example: Instead of a vague objective like "Improve sales," a specific objective would be "Increase quarterly sales by 15% in the North American region."

Measurable Key Results:

Key Results should be quantifiable and provide a clear measure of progress towards the objective.

Example: For the objective "Increase quarterly sales by 15% in the North American region," key results could be "Sign 10 new contracts with key accounts," "Increase average deal size by 10%," and "Reduce sales cycle time by 20%."

Challenging yet Achievable:

OKRs should be ambitious to drive high performance but also realistic enough to be achievable.

Example: An ambitious yet achievable objective could be "Launch three new product features that drive user engagement by 25%."

Time-Bound:

OKRs should have a clear timeline to ensure urgency and focus.

Example: Setting an objective to "Improve customer support response time by 50% in Q3" provides a specific timeframe for achieving the goal.

Tracking Progress and Performance

Tracking progress and performance is critical to measuring success with OKRs. This involves regular check-ins, updates, and reviews to ensure that teams stay on track and can make necessary adjustments. Here are key steps to effective tracking:

Regular Check-Ins:

Schedule regular check-ins (e.g., weekly or bi-weekly) to review progress, discuss challenges, and adjust plans as needed.

Example: A weekly team meeting to review OKR progress can help identify any obstacles early and ensure timely course corrections.

Use of OKR Software:

Leverage OKR software to track progress, provide visibility, and facilitate communication.

Example: Tools like Asana, WorkBoard, and Gtmhub can provide dashboards and reports that make it easy to track OKRs and share updates across the organization.

Scoring OKRs:

At the end of each OKR cycle, score each key result to evaluate success.

Example: Use a scoring system (e.g., 0-1.0 scale) where 0.7-1.0 indicates substantial achievement, 0.4-0.6 partial achievement, and 0.0-0.3 limited achievement.

Qualitative Feedback:

Supplement quantitative scores with qualitative feedback to provide context and insights.

Example: In addition to scoring, teams can provide narrative feedback on what went well, challenges faced, and lessons learned.

Continuous Improvement and Iteration

OKRs are not a one-time activity but a continuous cycle of setting, tracking, evaluating, and refining. Here's how to embed continuous improvement into your OKR process:

End-of-Cycle Evaluations:

Conduct thorough evaluations at the end of each OKR cycle to assess performance and identify areas for improvement.

Example: After a quarterly OKR cycle, hold a review meeting to discuss what objectives were met, which key results were most impactful, and any unexpected challenges.

Reflect and Learn:

Use retrospectives to reflect on the OKR process and outcomes, identifying key learnings and areas for enhancement.

Example: In a retrospective meeting, teams can discuss what went well, what didn't, and agree on 2-3 improvements for the next cycle.

Adjust and Refine:

Use the insights from evaluations and retrospectives to adjust and refine your OKRs for the next cycle.

Example: If a sales team found that one key result was too ambitious, they might set a more realistic target in the next cycle while maintaining a focus on ambitious growth.

Overcoming Common Challenges

Implementing and measuring success with OKRs can present challenges. Here's how to overcome some common obstacles:

Misalignment of Goals:

Challenge: Misalignment between individual, team, and organizational OKRs can lead to fragmented efforts.

Solution: Ensure alignment by cascading OKRs and regularly reviewing alignment during check-ins.

Example: Use OKR alignment meetings to ensure that team OKRs support the overall strategic objectives.

Lack of Engagement:

Challenge: Low engagement and buy-in from employees can hinder the effectiveness of OKRs.

Solution: Involve employees in the OKR-setting process and communicate the benefits of OKRs.

Example: Conduct workshops and training sessions to educate employees on the OKR process and its impact on their roles and the organization.

Inconsistent Tracking and Reporting:

Challenge: Inconsistent tracking and reporting can lead to a lack of visibility and accountability.

Solution: Use OKR software to standardize tracking and reporting, and ensure regular check-ins.

Example: Implement a weekly OKR review process using an OKR tracking tool to maintain consistency and visibility.

Setting Unrealistic OKRs:

Challenge: Setting overly ambitious OKRs can lead to frustration and burnout.

Solution: Balance ambition with realism, and ensure that OKRs are challenging yet achievable.

Example: Review past performance and capabilities when setting OKRs to ensure they are ambitious but realistic.

Real-World Examples of OKR Success

To illustrate the power of OKRs, let's look at some real-world examples of organizations that have successfully implemented OKRs and measured their success:

Google:

Overview: Google is known for its rigorous use of OKRs to drive innovation and growth.

Example: One of Google's early OKRs was to "Organize the world's information and make it universally accessible and useful," with key results focused on launching new search features and improving search accuracy.

Outcome: This OKR helped Google focus its efforts on improving its search engine, leading to its dominance in the search market.

Intel:

Overview: Intel, the originator of the OKR framework, has used OKRs to drive strategic initiatives and improve performance.

Example: Intel set an objective to "Achieve 90% market share in the microprocessor market," with key results focused on increasing production capacity, improving product performance, and expanding marketing efforts.

Outcome: This OKR helped Intel focus its resources on key areas, leading to significant market share gains.

<u>Spotify:</u>

Overview: Spotify uses OKRs to drive innovation and improve user experience.

Example: Spotify set an objective to "Increase user engagement by 20%," with key results focused on launching new features, improving app performance, and enhancing personalized recommendations.

Outcome: This OKR helped Spotify focus on user-centric improvements, leading to increased user engagement and satisfaction.

Conclusion

Implementing and measuring success with OKRs can transform your organization, aligning efforts, driving accountability, and fostering a culture of continuous improvement. As a CEO, your commitment to the OKR process can ignite the collective energy of your employees, much like a magnifying glass focuses the sun's rays to create powerful results. By setting clear, measurable OKRs, tracking progress diligently, and continuously refining your approach, you can steer your organization toward its strategic goals with precision and purpose.

Now is the time to implement OKRs with urgency, right earnest, and total belief. By doing so, you will empower your employees, drive organizational success, and ensure that every action taken within your organization contributes to its long-term vision. The journey to achieving your goals begins with the first step of setting and measuring your OKRs – take that step with confidence and determination, and watch your organization soar to new heights.

CHAPTER NINETEEN

CEO'S best practices for Objective setting

Achieving exceptional execution of company plans requires a clear distinction between outcomes and efforts. Here's how OKRs (Objectives and Key Results) serve as a powerful framework to ensure this:

Understanding Outcomes vs. Efforts

Outcomes: These are the results you aim to achieve. In a sports analogy, if you're a cricket coach, your outcome is winning the championship.

Efforts: These are the actions that lead to achieving those outcomes. For the cricket coach, efforts include recruiting players, conducting training sessions, and enhancing the effectiveness of assistant coaches.

Similarly, for a company aiming to grow its revenue 10x, efforts would include recruiting the right people, planning to achieve strategic goals, meeting sales and marketing targets, enhancing customer satisfaction, and launching new products.

Strategic Goals and Execution

CEOs and leadership teams make strategic bets to achieve desired growth. These bets, or strategic goals, are where OKRs come into play. However, many companies struggle with execution because they lack a process to:

Link Outcomes (Key KPIs) and Efforts (Action Plan) to Company Objectives (Strategic Goals): This ensures that every action is aligned with the broader company goals.

Enable People to Think in Terms of Quality Outcomes and Action Plans: This fosters a results-oriented mindset.

Set a Cadence of Review: Regular reviews keep everyone focused on outcomes and efforts.

Common Pitfalls in Execution

Many organizations fail to execute their strategic plans effectively for several reasons:

Plans Are Not Designed for Delivery and Execution: They remain abstract and unrelatable for most employees.

Lack of Engagement Beyond Leadership: Few people can translate strategic goals into actionable tasks.

Absence of a Repeatable Process: Many companies lack a simple, flexible process for creating and executing plans.

Inflexibility to Adjust to Changes: Plans often fail to adapt to changing market conditions or internal dynamics.

How OKRs Help

The OKR framework addresses these challenges by:

Defining Key KPIs (Outcomes) and Related Action Plans (Efforts): This ensures every team member understands what needs to be achieved and how to achieve it.

Linking These to Company Objectives (Strategic Goals): This alignment accelerates growth and ensures everyone is working towards the same goals.

Key Components of OKRs

Objectives: Clear, specific goals that are ambitious yet achievable.

Example: "Increase quarterly sales by 15% in the North American region."

Key Results: Measurable milestones that indicate progress towards the objective.

Example: "Sign 10 new contracts with key accounts," "Increase average deal size by 10%," and "Reduce sales cycle time by 20%."

Ensuring Buy-In and Successful OKR Implementation by Engaged Business Heads for OKR Success:

Securing Buy-In for OKRs Once the core OKR team has established the big-arrow and company objectives, gaining buy-in from business heads is crucial. This involves:

Big-Arrow and Objectives: Ensuring alignment and understanding of the overarching goals.

OKR Initiative: Explaining the value and process of implementing OKRs.

Review Cadence: Integrating regular review meetings with OKR tracking.

The CEO should lead an OKR workshop to explain the significance of the big-arrow, company objectives, and OKRs. This buy-in is essential as business heads may resist change initially. When they comprehend the importance of OKRs, they can champion the initiative within their teams, fostering widespread acceptance.

Common Challenges During implementation: It is common to witness intense discussions among leadership about the company's 12-month goals. Surprisingly, even established companies often struggle to align on this process. Following the CEO-led session, business heads should conduct similar workshops with their teams to reinforce the importance and process of OKRs.

Key Learning: Getting buy-in from business heads and their teams is the second critical step in OKR implementation.

3 Steps to Define Objectives Every Quarter

Step 1: Team Collaboration

Action: Quarterly, the functional head leads a session where the team collaborates to create a list of potential objectives that can be achieved in the upcoming quarter.

Step 2: Assess Impact

Action: Evaluate each candidate objective by scoring its impact on the company's overall objectives (as defined by the CEO) with ratings of "High," "Medium," or "Low."

Step 3: Finalize Objectives

Action: From the list of candidate objectives, select 2 to 3 high-impact objectives to focus on. While the number of objectives can sometimes reach up to 7, this often indicates that the company is either a growing startup trying to achieve product-market fit, needs to hire more staff, or is overextending efforts without prioritizing the most impactful goals.

Checklist for Finalized Objectives:

Alignment: Each objective should align with only one company objective.

Impact: The objective should have the highest impact on achieving the company objective.

Clarity and Inspiration: The objective statement should be simple to understand and inspirational.

Timeliness: The due date for achieving the objective should be on or before the quarter-end date.

Common Mistakes to Avoid When Defining Company Objectives

1. Ensure Uniqueness to Your Company

Avoid creating objectives that are so generic that they could apply to any competitor if their logo were swapped in. Your objectives should be unique to your company's mission and goals.

2. Keep Objectives Clear and Understandable

Explanation: Objectives should be simple and easy to understand. If the statement is too complex, it can cause confusion and make it difficult for the team to relate to and rally behind.

3. Limit the Number of Objectives

Explanation: Don't overextend by defining too many objectives. Focus on 3 to 4 key objectives to ensure that efforts are concentrated on what matters most and that resources are effectively allocated.

4. Separate Objectives from Key Results

Explanation: Do not include key results (the specific, measurable steps to achieve the objectives) within the company objectives. Objectives are broader goals to be achieved within the next 12 months, while key results are the milestones that track progress towards these goals.

5. Collaborate with Leadership

As a CEO, don't unilaterally decide on the company objectives. Engage in brainstorming sessions with your leadership team to ensure that the objectives are well-rounded, realistic, and have buy-in from all key stakeholders. This collaborative approach enhances alignment and commitment across the organization.

3 Steps to Define Key Results for Selected Objectives

Step 1: Start with one high-impact objective from your list.

Focus on a single objective at a time to maintain clarity and precision.

Step 2: Define 1 or 2 outcome-based key results.

These key results should indicate the measurable outcomes you aim to achieve.

Step 3: Identify effort-based key results to support the outcomes.

Determine the specific actions or efforts needed to achieve the defined outcomes.

Step 4: Assign an owner to each key result.

Ensure each key result has a clearly identified owner responsible for its achievement.

Step 5: Repeat the process for the next high-impact objective.

Move on to the next objective and define its key results similarly.

Checklist for Effective Key Results

Simplicity: Key results should be easy to understand and act upon.

Ownership: Each key result should have only one owner.

Relevance: Ensure that measuring the key result is worthwhile and meaningful.

Mistakes to Avoid

Mistake 1: Delaying the Definition Process

Avoid failing to define objectives and key results every quarter or taking too long (25-30 days) after a new quarter starts. The OKR process owner should remind and follow up with managers to set them every quarter, especially for the first four cycles.

Mistake 2: Rushing the Process

Don't rush through defining key results. Stick to the agenda and allocate sufficient time (typically 120-180 minutes for a team of 4-6) to complete the process.

Mistake 3: Overloading Key Results

Avoid defining too many effort-based and outcome-based key results. Focus on the most critical ones.

Mistake 4: Lack of Communication

Ensure you communicate with team members who will own key results from other teams before assigning them. This helps in getting their buy-in and commitment.

By following these steps and avoiding common pitfalls, you can effectively define key results that drive progress and align with your high-impact objectives.

Committed and Aspirational Key Results in OKRs

In the OKR framework, key results are classified into two categories: committed and aspirational. This distinction helps organizations balance achievable goals with ambitious targets that drive innovation and maintain agility.

1. Committed Key Results:

Definition: These are specific, realistic, and achievable targets that the team is expected to meet within the set time frame.

Purpose: Committed key results ensure that essential, day-to-day business operations and incremental improvements are accomplished. They provide a stable foundation for performance and reliability.

Example: "Increase customer satisfaction score from 70% to 80% by the end of Q2."

2. Aspirational Key Results:

Definition: These are ambitious, challenging targets that push the team beyond its current capabilities. Achieving these may seem difficult, but they are designed to inspire and stretch the team's potential.

Purpose: Aspirational key results foster a culture of innovation and continuous improvement. They encourage employees to think creatively and take calculated risks.

Example: "Double the number of active users on the platform in the next six months."

How Committed and Aspirational Key Results Facilitate Organizational Agility and Innovation

1. Encouraging a Balanced Approach:

Stability and Growth: Committed key results ensure that the organization continues to deliver reliable performance and meets essential business targets. This stability allows the organization to maintain its operational effectiveness.

Innovation and Agility: Aspirational key results encourage teams to explore new ideas and approaches, pushing boundaries and fostering a culture of innovation. This balance helps organizations remain agile and responsive to changes.

2. Driving Continuous Improvement:

Setting High Expectations: Aspirational key results challenge employees to exceed their usual performance levels, fostering a mindset of continuous improvement.

Learning from Failures: Even if aspirational targets are not fully met, the pursuit of these goals leads to valuable insights and learning opportunities that drive future success.

3. Preserving Entrepreneurial Spirit:

Empowerment and Ownership: By setting ambitious goals, employees feel empowered to take ownership of their work and contribute to the company's vision. This sense of responsibility helps preserve the entrepreneurial spirit within the organization.

Risk-Taking Culture: Encouraging aspirational key results promotes a culture where calculated risks are valued, and innovative ideas are pursued. This risk-taking culture is essential for long-term growth and maintaining a competitive edge.

4. Examples from Leading Companies:

Google: Google famously uses aspirational OKRs to push the limits of innovation. For example, its ambitious goals for its search engine and other products have led to significant breakthroughs and industry leadership.

Intel: Intel's use of OKRs has helped it navigate the rapidly changing tech industry. By balancing committed results with aspirational targets, Intel has continued to innovate and stay ahead of competitors.

By integrating both committed and aspirational key results, organizations can effectively manage their current operations while also striving for innovative growth. This dual approach ensures that companies remain agile, continuously improve, and maintain an entrepreneurial spirit, much like leading companies such as Google and Intel. Embracing this balance is key to sustaining long-term success and competitiveness in today's dynamic business environment.

CHAPTER TWENTY

CEOs guide to a Successful OKR implementation

Implementing Objectives and Key Results (OKRs) successfully can transform the way a company operates, driving focus, alignment, and measurable progress. The journey to effective OKR adoption involves more than just setting ambitious goals; it requires a structured approach, cultural shift, and committed leadership. This chapter delves into the critical elements that constitute a successful OKR implementation, offering a roadmap for organizations looking to harness the power of this strategic framework.

From securing buy-in from key stakeholders to establishing a sustainable review cadence, each aspect is crucial in embedding OKRs into the fabric of the organization. By understanding the anatomy of successful OKR implementation, companies can navigate challenges, optimize their goal-setting practices, and ultimately achieve greater agility and performance.

<u>Four Principles for Successful OKR Implementation</u>

Define Few Important Objectives Each Quarter: Focus on a limited number of crucial goals.

Set Key Results and Action Plans: Outline specific outcomes (KPIs) and efforts required to achieve these objectives.

Integrate Business Reviews with OKRs: Align regular business reviews with OKR updates to maintain focus and accountability.

Enhance Managerial Effectiveness: Ensure managers are equipped to set impactful outcomes and action plans.

<u>Stages of OKR Implementation:</u> Implementing OKRs requires a cultural shift, prompting individuals to think, plan, and articulate their quarterly goals. Successful OKR adoption can establish a cadence where teams regularly meet, plan, and execute strategies for business growth, rather than just performing daily tasks without a clear connection to overall objectives.

Stage 1: Learn & Create

Duration: 9 to 15 months.

Activities: All levels, from the CEO to managers, learn about OKRs, creating company objectives and corresponding key results. This stage fosters clarity on the company's goals and individual contributions.

Stage 2: Adopt & Optimize

Duration: Post 15 months.

Activities: Teams start seeing the impact of OKRs, experiencing enhanced transparency, collaboration, and execution speed. Resistance decreases, and quarterly OKR definitions and reviews become routine. Objectives and key results are refined for greater impact, and the CEO gains insights into the effectiveness of strategic initiatives.

Key Learning: Successful OKR implementation hinges on widespread buy-in, adherence to core principles, and navigating through the learning and optimization stages.

The Process of Implementing OKRs

Setting Clear Goals: Define what success looks like.

Example: A CEO decides that the objective for the next quarter is to enhance customer satisfaction.

Defining Scope and Parameters: Outline the boundaries and expectations.

Example: The scope includes improving customer support response time and overall user experience.

Selecting a Pilot Group: Start small to refine the process.

Example: Begin with the customer support team to test the new strategies.

Getting All Important People on Board: Ensure buy-in from key stakeholders.

Example: Involve the heads of customer support, product development, and marketing.

Training Participants and Stakeholders: Educate everyone on the OKR framework.

Example: Conduct workshops and training sessions for the customer support team.

Implementing the First OKR Cycle: Execute the plan with the pilot group.

Example: The customer support team begins using OKRs to improve response times.

Reflecting on the Pilot Project: Assess what worked and what didn't.

Example: After the first quarter, review the results and gather feedback from the team.

Planning the Rollout: Expand the implementation based on the pilot's success.

Example: Roll out the OKR process to the entire customer service department, then to other departments.

Embedding OKRs into Company Culture

Every company aims to be the best, but many struggle to create a culture of discipline where teams can determine, with egoless clarity, what outcomes they can achieve and commit to doing whatever it takes to achieve them. OKRs can help foster this culture by:

Focusing on Outcomes, Not Just Efforts: Ensure everyone understands the results they need to achieve.

Making It a Continuous Process: Avoid treating OKRs as just another goal-setting exercise. Instead, integrate them into the daily routine and review them regularly to keep them relevant and top-of-mind.

<u>The Importance of Mindset</u>

For OKR implementation to be successful, it must be seen as a tool for making things happen and achieving desired outcomes. If people perceive it as merely another goal-setting exercise done quarterly, there is a high chance of failure. The right mindset is crucial:

Quality Thinking and Planning: Encourage teams to think critically about their goals and how to achieve them.

Continuous Improvement: Regular reviews and adjustments help keep plans relevant and achievable.

Key Insight: OKR is a framework for CEOs and companies to align Outcomes (Key KPIs) and Efforts (Action Plans) with Company Objectives. It fosters a culture of strategic thinking, meticulous planning, and consistent achievement within teams.

Conclusion

OKRs transform strategic goals into actionable plans, ensuring that efforts are focused on achieving specific, measurable outcomes. This structured approach not only drives accountability and transparency but also fosters a culture of continuous improvement. By implementing

OKRs with urgency and commitment, CEOs can ignite the collective energy of their employees, much like a magnifying glass focuses the sun's rays to create powerful results. This alignment and focus enable organizations to achieve their goals with precision and purpose, ensuring sustained growth and success.

CHAPTER TWENTY-ONE

New Dimensions & Advances in OKR strategies

As organizations mature in their use of OKRs (Objectives and Key Results), they often seek more sophisticated strategies to enhance their effectiveness and drive even greater performance. Advanced OKR strategies go beyond the basics of setting and tracking objectives and delve into nuanced approaches that foster deeper alignment, engagement, and adaptability. Here, we explore several advanced strategies, their implementation, and the benefits they bring.

1. **Integrating OKRs with Performance Management**

The integration of OKRs (Objectives and Key Results) with performance assessments and rewards is a debated topic in the realm of goal-setting and performance management. The common consensus in the literature is to avoid directly linking OKRs with rewards. At qilo, we have a nuanced perspective on this matter.

The Case Against Direct Linkage

Linking OKRs directly with rewards can lead to conservative goal-setting. When employees know that their compensation is tied to the achievement of their key results, they are less likely to set ambitious, stretch goals. This behavior can stifle innovation and risk-taking, essential components for driving growth and achieving significant breakthroughs.

The Need for Motivation and Recognition

On the other hand, if employees see no tangible benefit from the effort they put into defining and executing OKRs, their motivation can wane. It's crucial to answer the question, "What's in it for me?" for those who are driving the OKR process and achieving their targets. Recognition and rewards play a vital role in maintaining motivation and engagement.

Need for a Balanced Approach

We believe the solution lies in a balanced approach. OKRs should act as an input in the performance assessment and reward decisions but should not be the sole determinant. Here's how this balanced approach can be implemented:

Initial Focus on Process and Adoption:

For the first four quarters of implementing OKRs, the emphasis should be on setting the right kind of OKRs and establishing a routine for reviewing them.

During this period, do not directly link OKRs with rewards. Instead, focus on recognizing and celebrating OKR champions—those who excel in setting, executing, and living the OKR methodology. Ensure these recognitions are communicated company-wide to reinforce the importance of OKRs.

Gradual Integration with Performance Assessments:

After the initial four quarters, begin to incorporate OKR performance as one of the inputs for performance assessments and rewards.

Use the OKR score as a part of the overall evaluation process to determine rewards, but not the sole criterion. This allows for a holistic view of an employee's performance, considering both their achievement of key results and other factors such as teamwork, innovation, and overall contribution to the company.

Avoid Overemphasis on Rewards:

Ensure that the primary motivation for pursuing OKRs remains intrinsic—aligned with the company's mission, vision, and values—rather than extrinsic rewards alone.

Maintain a culture where achieving stretch goals and driving significant impact is valued and recognized, beyond just the financial rewards.

Practical Implementation Tips

Recognize Early Adopters: During the initial phase, identify and celebrate those who are adopting and excelling in the OKR process. This can be done through public acknowledgments, awards, or non-monetary rewards.

Regular Communication: Keep the entire organization informed about the importance of OKRs and the progress being made. Transparency in how OKRs are linked to performance assessments can help in setting the right expectations.

Continuous Feedback: Provide regular feedback to employees on their OKR performance, helping them understand where they excel and where improvements are needed. This fosters a culture of continuous improvement and learning.

Linking OKRs with performance assessments and rewards requires a thoughtful and balanced approach.

Initially, focus on embedding the OKR process and creating a culture of goal-oriented execution. Gradually, integrate OKR performance into the broader performance assessment framework, ensuring it acts as one of the inputs rather than the sole determinant. By doing so, organizations can motivate employees to aim high, foster innovation, and drive significant business outcomes, while also recognizing and rewarding their efforts appropriately.

2. Utilizing Cross-Functional OKRs

Explanation: Cross-functional OKRs involve setting objectives that require collaboration across different departments or teams. This approach breaks down silos and encourages a more cohesive effort towards shared goals.

Example: An objective to "Improve customer satisfaction by 20%" might involve the customer service, product development, and marketing teams working together to enhance customer experience and address pain points.

Benefit: Promotes teamwork and ensures that complex goals, which require multiple perspectives and skills, are achieved more effectively.

3. Dynamic OKR Adjustments

Explanation: Dynamic OKR adjustments allow organizations to remain flexible and responsive to changes in the business environment. Instead of rigidly sticking to set OKRs, teams can modify their objectives and key results as new information and challenges arise.

Example: A tech company might adjust its OKRs mid-quarter if a major market shift occurs, such as the emergence of a new competitor or a significant change in customer preferences.

Benefit: Maintains relevance and agility, ensuring that OKRs remain aligned with current business priorities and external conditions.

4. Embedding OKRs in Daily Operations

Explanation: Embedding OKRs into daily operations involves making OKR tracking and progress a part of everyday activities. This means integrating OKR discussions into regular meetings, using OKR software for daily task management, and continuously referring to OKRs in decision-making processes.

Example: Teams might start each day with a brief meeting to discuss progress on key results and identify any obstacles, ensuring that daily tasks are always aligned with strategic objectives.

Benefit: Keeps OKRs at the forefront of employees' minds, fostering continuous alignment and focus on strategic goals.

5. Leveraging OKR Software Analytics

Explanation: Advanced OKR software often includes powerful analytics capabilities that provide insights into OKR progress, identify trends, and highlight areas needing attention. Leveraging these analytics can help organizations make data-driven decisions to improve OKR outcomes.

Example: An organization might use software analytics to identify which key results are lagging behind and then investigate the causes, such as resource constraints or misaligned priorities.

Benefit: Enables proactive management and continuous improvement by providing a clear, data-driven view of OKR performance.

6. OKR Coaching and Mentorship Programs

Explanation: Implementing coaching and mentorship programs for OKRs involves assigning experienced OKR champions or external consultants to guide teams and individuals in setting, tracking, and achieving their OKRs.

Example: New teams might be paired with a seasoned OKR coach who helps them refine their objectives and key results, ensuring they are ambitious yet achievable and aligned with company goals.

Benefit: Improves the quality of OKRs and boosts the likelihood of successful implementation through expert guidance and support.

7. Continuous Learning and Adaptation

Explanation: Fostering a culture of continuous learning and adaptation means regularly reflecting on OKR processes and outcomes to identify what works and what doesn't. This involves conducting retrospectives, gathering feedback, and iterating on OKR practices.

Example: After each OKR cycle, a company might hold a retrospective meeting where teams discuss their successes and challenges, share lessons learned, and propose improvements for the next cycle.

Benefit: Ensures that the OKR process evolves and improves over time, leading to better alignment, execution, and results.

Conclusion

Advanced OKR strategies can significantly enhance the impact of OKRs by fostering deeper alignment, improving collaboration, and ensuring agility in a rapidly changing business environment. By integrating OKRs with performance management, utilizing cross-functional objectives, allowing dynamic adjustments, embedding OKRs in daily operations, leveraging analytics, implementing coaching programs, and fostering continuous learning, organizations can drive sustained performance and achieve

CHAPTER TWENTY-TWO

OKR Tools, Software & Resources

To streamline the OKR process and ensure consistency across the organization, utilizing the right tools and software is essential. The book discusses various OKR management tools, highlighting their features, benefits, and integration capabilities. These tools help in setting, tracking, and reviewing OKRs, ensuring transparency and alignment throughout the company.

Popular OKR Tools:

Qilo: An intuitive platform co-founded by Vikram Kohli, designed to facilitate OKR implementation and alignment.

People Strong: Post-acquisition, Qilo's technology is integrated into People Strong's suite, offering a robust solution for performance management and OKR tracking.

WorkBoard: A comprehensive tool that provides strategic priorities and OKR alignment, along with execution management.

Ally.io: A software solution that helps organizations link OKRs to their strategic objectives and track progress in real-time.

Weekdone: A user-friendly platform focused on team alignment and productivity through OKRs.

OKR (Objectives and Key Results) software: OKR Software is essential for managing the OKR implementation process efficiently and effectively, particularly as organizations scale. The use of specialized software tools can streamline the setting, tracking, and reviewing of OKRs, ensuring alignment and engagement across all levels of the organization. Here's why OKR software is crucial and some key tools available in the market.

Benefits of Using OKR Software

Centralized Management:

OKR software provides a single platform where all objectives and key results are managed, making it easy to track progress and alignment across the organization.

Example: With centralized dashboards, managers can quickly see the status of team and organizational OKRs, ensuring everyone is on the same page.

Real-Time Tracking and Updates:

Real-time tracking ensures that progress on OKRs is updated continuously, allowing for timely interventions and adjustments.

Example: Teams can update their key results in real-time, providing immediate visibility to stakeholders and enabling quick responses to any deviations.

Enhanced Collaboration:

OKR software fosters collaboration by providing tools for communication, feedback, and cross-functional alignment.

Example: Teams can comment on OKRs, share updates, and discuss progress directly within the software, enhancing collaborative efforts.

Automated Reminders and Notifications:

Automated reminders and notifications help keep teams on track, ensuring that OKR reviews and updates happen regularly.

Example: Weekly reminders to update progress or review OKRs help maintain consistent focus and engagement.

Data-Driven Insights:

OKR software provides analytical tools to generate insights and reports, helping organizations make data-driven decisions.

Example: Analytics dashboards can show trends, identify bottlenecks, and highlight areas needing attention, guiding strategic decisions.

Scalability:

Explanation: OKR software is designed to scale with the organization, accommodating more users, objectives, and complexity as the organization grows.

A growing company can seamlessly add new teams and objectives without disrupting the existing OKR framework.

Key OKR Software Tools

OKR software tools are essential for organizations looking to streamline their goal-setting processes, track progress, and boost productivity. Here is a detailed analysis of some of the best OKR tools available in 2024, highlighting their standout features, best use cases, and pricing structures. Please note the following details are subject to change and updated information can be found from the respective websites or information portals and landing pages.

1. ClickUp

Best For: OKR project management

Standout Features: ClickUp Goals with trackable targets

Customizable OKR templates

ClickUp Brain (available on any paid plan for $5/member per Workspace per month)

Pricing:

Free Forever

Unlimited: $7/user per month

Business: $12/user per month

Enterprise: Contact for pricing

Analysis: ClickUp is a versatile tool that excels in OKR project management with its comprehensive goal tracking and customizable templates. The additional ClickUp Brain feature enhances its usability for advanced users.

2. Weekdone:

Overview: Weekdone provides a straightforward platform for managing OKRs, emphasizing simplicity and ease of use.

Features: Weekly check-ins, progress reports, team alignment tools.

Benefits: Encourages regular updates and team collaboration, making it ideal for smaller teams or companies new to OKRs.

Best For: Measuring weekly progress

Standout Features: Daily newsfeed, Weekly updates

Pricing: Free

Premium: Starting at $108/month (10-user package, $10.80/user/month)

Analysis: Weekdone focuses on weekly progress measurement, making it ideal for teams that require regular updates and engagement. Its daily newsfeed and weekly updates keep everyone on track.

3. Workboard

Best For: Improving team productivity

Standout Features: Smart agendas

Pricing: Not available (NA)

Analysis: Workboard enhances team productivity with smart agendas, though detailed pricing information is not provided. It is best suited for teams that prioritize structured meeting agendas and productivity improvements.

4. Lattice

Best For: Performance management and employee engagement

Standout Features: Continuous feedback

Pricing:

Performance Management + OKRs & Goals: $11/month per user

Engagement: +$4/month per user

Grow: +$4/month per user

Compensation: +$6/month per user

Analysis: Lattice offers a robust solution for performance management and employee engagement, with a focus on continuous feedback. Its modular pricing allows organizations to choose features that best meet their needs.

5. 15Five

Overview: 15Five integrates OKRs with continuous performance management, including feedback, recognition, and one-on-one meetings.

Features: Continuous feedback, performance reviews, recognition tools.

Benefits: Enhances employee engagement and performance alongside OKR tracking

Best For: Feedback-based OKR tracking

Standout Features: Best-self review dashboard, High-fives

Pricing:

Engage: $4/month per user (annual billing only)

Perform: $10/month per user (annual billing only)

Total Platform: $16/month per user (annual billing only)

Analysis: 15Five is designed for feedback-based OKR tracking with features that promote positive reinforcement and self-improvement. The best-self review dashboard is a standout feature for fostering employee development.

6. Asana

Best For: Project and task management

Standout Features: Visual progress tracking, Numerous integrations

Pricing:

Free

Starter: $13.49/month per user

Advanced: $30.49/month per user

Enterprise: Custom pricing

Enterprise+: Custom pricing

Analysis: Asana is a comprehensive project and task management tool with excellent visual progress tracking and integration capabilities. It is suitable for teams of all sizes, especially those managing complex projects.

7. Betterworks

Overview: Betterworks offers enterprise-grade OKR management with advanced features for goal setting, tracking, and performance management.

Features: Goal cascading, real-time feedback, performance insights.

Benefits: Suitable for large organizations needing comprehensive OKR management and performance tracking

Best For: Feedback and communication

Standout Features: Unbiased calibrations

Pricing:

Enterprise: Custom pricing

Mid-Market: Custom pricing

Analysis: Betterworks excels in providing unbiased calibrations and fostering effective feedback and communication within teams. It is ideal for medium to large enterprises seeking customized solutions.

8. Peoplebox

Best For: Building a high-performance culture

Standout Features: Team alignment insights

Pricing:

Talent Management: $7/month per user (annual billing only)

OKR Platform: $8/month per user (annual billing only)

Full-Suite Professional: $12/month per user (annual billing only)

Full-Suite Premium: $15/month per user (annual billing only)

Enterprise Plan: Custom pricing

Analysis: Peoplebox offers insights into team alignment, making it valuable for companies aiming to build a high-performance culture. Its comprehensive pricing plans cater to various organizational needs.

9. PerformYard

Best For: Customizable performance reviews

Standout Features: Flexible goal cascading, Customizable review cycles

Pricing:

Performance Management: $5-$10/month per user (annual billing only)

Employee Engagement: Starting at $1-$3/month per user (annual billing only)

Analysis: PerformYard provides flexible and customizable performance reviews, ideal for organizations needing tailored review processes. Its scalable pricing makes it accessible for both small and large teams.

10. Hirebook

Best For: Boosting employee engagement

Standout Features: Detailed org charts

Pricing:

Business: $15/month per user

Enterprise: Custom pricing

Analysis: Hirebook focuses on boosting employee engagement with features like detailed organizational charts. It is suitable for businesses looking to enhance internal communication and engagement.

11. Quantive Results

Best For: Benchmarking reports

Standout Features: Achievement highlights, OKR version history

Pricing:

Essentials: Free

Scale: $9/month per user

Enterprise: Custom Pricing

Analysis: Quantive Results is excellent for organizations that need benchmarking reports and historical OKR data. Its free plan provides basic functionalities, while the Scale and Enterprise plans offer more advanced features.

12. Kallidus Perform

Best For: Learning and development and employee lifecycle management

Standout Features: Multi-level OKR tracking

Pricing: Custom pricing

Analysis: Kallidus Perform integrates learning and development with OKR tracking, ideal for organizations focusing on employee growth and lifecycle management. Custom pricing allows for tailored solutions.

13. Profit.co

Best For: Customizable OKR management

Standout Features:

400+ in-built and custom KPIs

Visual dashboard

Pricing: Custom pricing

Analysis: Profit.co offers extensive customization for OKR management with numerous in-built KPIs and a visual dashboard. It suits organizations that require detailed and flexible OKR tracking.

14. Viva Goals

Best For: Goal setting and tracking using templates

Standout Features:

Ready-to-use presentation frameworks for PowerPoint

Pricing:

Microsoft Viva in Microsoft 365: Available as part of Microsoft 365 enterprise plan

Microsoft Viva Employee Communications and Communities: $2/month per user (annual billing only)

Microsoft Viva Workplace Analytics and Employee Feedback: $6/month per user (annual billing only)

Microsoft Viva Suite: $12/month per user (annual billing only)

Analysis: Viva Goals, integrated with Microsoft 365, is ideal for goal setting and tracking with pre-made templates. It is perfect for organizations already using Microsoft's ecosystem.

15. Mooncamp

Best For: Hierarchical strategy designing

Standout Features: Strategy tree

Pricing:

Essential: $6/month per user (annual billing only)

Professional: $10/month per user (annual billing only)

Enterprise: Custom pricing

Analysis: Mooncamp's strategy tree feature supports hierarchical strategy designing, making it suitable for companies needing structured and visual strategic planning.

16. Gtmhub:

Overview: Gtmhub offers robust features for setting and tracking OKRs, including real-time data integration and automated insights.

Features: Data-driven insights, customizable dashboards, real-time tracking.

Benefits: Helps organizations link OKRs with business metrics for data-driven decision-making.

17. Perdoo:

Overview: Perdoo combines OKRs with strategic themes and goals, providing a comprehensive view of organizational performance.

Features: Strategic goal alignment, KPI tracking, progress visualization.

Benefits: Ensures alignment between daily activities and long-term strategic goals.

This analysis highlights the strengths and best use cases for each OKR software tool, along with their standout features and pricing. Organizations can choose the best tool based on their specific needs and requirements.

For a curated set of information for OKR implementation videos and guides, please visit **https://tinyurl.com/OKR-Resources**

CHAPTER TWENTY-THREE

Conclusion

OKRs (Objectives and Key Results) have emerged as a powerful framework for businesses, both small and large, to align their efforts, focus resources, and achieve ambitious goals. Looking ahead, the future of OKRs promises to further enhance organizational agility, performance, and societal impact.

Enhancing Business Focus and Resource Allocation

OKRs enable businesses to articulate clear objectives and measurable outcomes that guide resource allocation and strategic decision-making. By setting ambitious yet achievable goals, organizations can prioritize initiatives that drive growth, innovation, and operational excellence. This focus ensures that every employee's efforts contribute directly to overarching business objectives, thereby maximizing efficiency and effectiveness.

Converging Activities and Aligning Efforts

One of the key strengths of OKRs lies in their ability to converge the activities of all employees towards common goals. Whether in startups or large corporations, OKRs create alignment across departments and functions, fostering collaboration and synergy. This alignment ensures that everyone understands their role in achieving shared objectives, promoting a cohesive organizational culture centered on achievement and accountability.

Driving Success and Thriving in Competitive Markets

Businesses leveraging OKRs not only set goals but also continuously review and adjust them based on performance insights. This iterative process of setting, tracking, and adapting goals allows organizations to respond swiftly to market dynamics and changing customer needs. This adaptability is crucial for staying competitive and seizing opportunities in rapidly evolving industries.

Creating Value for Society

Beyond business success, OKRs have the potential to create significant value for society at large. When companies align their goals with broader societal needs and sustainability goals, OKRs become a tool for driving positive change. By integrating social responsibility into their objectives, businesses can contribute to environmental stewardship, community well-being, and ethical business practices, thereby enhancing their reputation and long-term viability.

The Road Ahead: Innovations and Applications

Looking forward, the evolution of OKRs is likely to include advancements in technology, data analytics, and predictive modeling. These innovations will enable more sophisticated goal-setting, real-time performance tracking, and predictive insights. Additionally, the integration of OKRs with AI-driven tools and automation will streamline processes, enhance decision-making, and drive operational efficiency.

Small Businesses and Startups

For small businesses and startups, OKRs offer a structured approach to scaling operations while maintaining clarity and alignment. By focusing on a few high-impact objectives, startups can prioritize growth initiatives and attract investment. OKRs also foster a culture of agility and innovation, essential for navigating uncertainties and seizing growth opportunities in competitive markets.

Large Corporations

In large corporations, OKRs facilitate strategic alignment across diverse divisions and geographies. They provide leadership with visibility into progress at all levels of the organization, enabling informed decision-making and course corrections. OKRs also promote employee engagement and motivation by aligning individual goals with organizational objectives, fostering a sense of purpose and achievement.

In this journey through the world of Objectives and Key Results (OKRs), we have explored a strategic framework that transcends mere goal-setting, offering a pathway to organizational alignment, growth, and sustainable success. OKRs serve as more than just a tool; they are a philosophy that aligns teams, focuses efforts, and drives performance towards achieving strategic objectives.

<u>Key Learnings and Takeaways:</u>

Alignment for Impact: OKRs excel in aligning individual aspirations with organizational goals. By cascading objectives from top-level strategic initiatives down to departmental and individual levels, OKRs ensure that every action contributes to the overall mission and vision of the organization.

Driving Accountability: Central to the success of OKRs is their ability to foster accountability. When teams take ownership of measurable Key Results tied to their Objectives, it instills a culture of responsibility and achievement. Regular review sessions and feedback loops enhance performance and keep teams on track.

Balancing Ambition and Realism: OKRs encourage setting ambitious goals while emphasizing the importance of feasibility and adaptability. This balance allows organizations to stretch their capabilities while remaining responsive to changing market dynamics and internal challenges.

Leadership and Culture: Effective leadership is critical in OKR implementation. Leaders play a pivotal role in communicating strategic priorities, supporting teams in achieving their OKRs, and reinforcing a culture of transparency, collaboration, and continuous improvement.

Rewarding Success: While caution is advised in directly linking OKRs to individual rewards, recognizing and celebrating achievements tied to OKRs fosters motivation and commitment. Rewards should reflect both quantitative outcomes and qualitative contributions towards organizational objectives.

Looking Forward:

As we look to the future, the evolution of OKRs will continue to shape organizational strategy and performance management. Advances in technology, data analytics, and remote collaboration tools will further enhance the effectiveness of OKRs in driving agility, innovation, and resilience in organizations of all sizes.

Final Thoughts:

ACT NOW- Objectives and Key Results to "Align for Growth" advocates for a strategic approach to OKRs—one that integrates organizational purpose, fosters alignment across diverse teams, and empowers individuals to contribute meaningfully towards shared goals. By embracing OKRs as a foundational element of organizational strategy, companies can navigate complexity with clarity, drive sustainable growth, and achieve enduring success in a competitive landscape.

As you embark on your OKR journey, remember that the true power of OKRs lies not only in setting goals but in aligning actions, inspiring teams, and achieving transformative results. Here's to leveraging OKRs to unlock potential, drive innovation, and create value for stakeholders, employees, and society at large.

Conclusion

In conclusion, the future of OKRs holds promise for businesses seeking to thrive in a dynamic and interconnected world. By leveraging OKRs to focus resources, converge activities, and drive organizational success, businesses can not only achieve their goals but also create significant societal value. As businesses embrace OKRs as a strategic imperative, they position themselves to lead with purpose, innovation, and sustainable growth in the years ahead.

While a lot of effort has gone into provide the esteemed readers with comprehensive, relevant and useful information, there could be some inadvertant errors and ommissions that could be corrected and improved upon. Kindly send us your feedbacks and suggestions to Srinivas Mahankali at email id: bct4nip@gmail.com.

Frequently Asked Questions (faq)

<u>Getting Started with OKRs</u>

1. Question: How do OKRs align with our overall strategy?

Answer: OKRs translate your strategic vision into actionable objectives and measurable results, ensuring that every team and individual in the organization is working towards the same strategic goals.

2. Question: Should the CEO and top management be involved in OKR implementation from the start? Answer: Yes, ideally, the implementation should start with the CEO and top management. Solving alignment issues at the top can lead to breakthroughs and set the tone for the rest of the organization.

3. Question: Who should lead the OKR implementation?

Answer: The ideal OKR Program Head should understand the company business horizontally and have the ability to influence people at all levels. For large companies, this could be the Strategy Head, Chief of Staff, COO, CHRO, or CEO. For SMBs and start-ups, it could be a functional head or a business performance specialist.

<u>OKR Implementation Process</u>

4. Question: What's the best strategy for rolling out OKRs in our organization?

Answer: The rollout strategy depends on the company culture. For companies with communication, trust, collaboration, and transparency issues, start small and implement OKRs at the top three levels: Management, Functional Heads, and Operational Managers. For growing start-ups or mid-sized businesses, OKRs can be rolled out across the company in one go.

5. Question: How can we ensure teams create quality OKRs, especially Key Results?

Answer: Provide thorough training on the OKR concept.

Regularly communicate guidelines for creating Objectives and Key Results and conducting reviews.

Use analytics to monitor the types of Key Results being created.

Reward and recognize those who draft effective OKRs and conduct regular reviews.

6. Question: Should OKRs be team-based or individual-based?

Answer: It depends on your company's culture and needs, but team-based OKRs generally work better. They reduce the number of objectives, enhance collaboration, and improve managers' coaching abilities.

7. Question: How can we manage resistance to OKR implementation from managers and employees? Answer: Understand why people are resisting change, listen to their concerns, share success stories, and communicate the behaviors and principles the company expects. Most will come on board with effective communication.

Reviews and Adaptation

8. Question: What are the challenges in conducting monthly OKR review sessions?

Answer: Challenges include managers not conducting reviews regularly, hijacking sessions, and sessions running over time. Fix a regular schedule, ensure team members share progress first, and find the right balance for time allocation.

9. Question: Why do managers frequently change Objectives and Key Results?

Answer: Initially, it might take managers 3-4 quarters to understand how to set the right objectives and Key Results. If changes happen frequently, discuss with the manager to understand their thought process.

10. Question: How do we measure the success of our OKR system?

Answer: Evaluate the success by assessing the achievement of Key Results, alignment with strategic goals, employee engagement, business performance, and the ability to adapt and improve the OKR process over time.

<u>**Advanced OKR Concepts**</u>

11. Question: How do OKRs differ from KPIs and KRAs?

Answer: OKRs focus on setting and achieving ambitious goals, integrating both KPIs (specific metrics to gauge performance) and KRAs (main areas of outcomes) into a framework that drives alignment and strategic focus.

12. Question: What is the FACTS-CFR approach in relation to OKRs?

Answer: The FACTS-CFR (Focus, Alignment, Commitment, Tracking, and Stretch – Conversation, Feedback, and Recognition) approach emphasizes focusing on key priorities, aligning efforts, committing to objectives, tracking progress, stretching for ambitious goals, and maintaining open communication, feedback, and recognition throughout the process.

13. Question: How do OKRs promote transparency in the organization?

Answer: OKRs make goals and progress visible to everyone, encouraging accountability, fostering trust, and enabling collaboration as everyone understands what others are working on and how it aligns with the company's objectives.

14. Question: Can OKRs improve employee engagement?

Answer: Yes, OKRs can significantly improve employee engagement by involving employees in the goal-setting process and providing clarity on how their work contributes to the company's success.

Strategic Alignment and Pivots

15. Question: How do OKRs support strategic pivots?

Answer: OKRs are flexible and adaptable, making them ideal for supporting strategic pivots. When the company's strategy changes, OKRs can be quickly realigned to reflect the new direction, ensuring all efforts are focused on the updated priorities.

16. Question: What are the benefits of setting stretch goals in OKRs?

Answer: Stretch goals push teams beyond their comfort zones, driving innovation, creativity, and a growth mindset. While not always fully achieved, striving towards them can lead to significant progress and breakthroughs.

17. Question: What should we consider when choosing an OKR software vendor? Answer:
Consider the vendor's implementation experience, support in process execution, integration capabilities, hosting preferences, data security, training provisions, ease of use, and the insights and reports the software offers.

Troubleshooting and Continuous Improvement

18. Question: What if we don't see results from OKRs after 12-15 months?

Answer: If OKRs aren't showing results, re-evaluate strategic bets, review execution strategies, and ensure OKRs aren't treated as mere goal-setting exercises. Seek expert help if needed to reassess your implementation approach.

19. Question: How can OKRs drive company-wide alignment? Answer:

OKRs create a clear line of sight from the company's strategic objectives to team and individual goals, ensuring everyone is working towards the same objectives and driving cohesive efforts.

20. Question: How do Key Results differ from to-do lists?

Answer: Key Results are metrics and high-level steps to achieve objectives, including numerical targets, progress milestones, or to-do items. To-dos/tasks are subsets of Key Results.

21. Question: How should we handle failures in achieving OKRs?

Answer: Treat failures as learning opportunities. Analyze what went wrong, understand the reasons, and use insights to improve future goal-setting and execution. Encourage a culture where it's safe to fail and learn.

Driving Adoption and Success

22. Question: How can we ensure that OKRs remain relevant and up-to-date?

Answer: Regularly review and update OKRs to align with strategic goals and respond to business changes. Encourage continuous feedback and make adjustments as needed.

23. Question: How can we get buy-in from all levels of the organization for OKRs?

Answer: Communicate the benefits, involve key stakeholders, provide comprehensive training, share success stories, and encourage active participation and feedback from all employees.

24. Question: What are the signs of a successful OKR implementation?

Answer: Successful implementation is indicated by clear alignment, increased engagement, regular reviews, visible progress, adaptability, and improved collaboration and communication across teams.

25. Question: How can OKRs help in resource allocation?

Answer: OKRs provide a clear framework for prioritizing work, ensuring resources are directed towards the most important and impactful areas, leading to better outcomes.

26. Question: What are the best practices for integrating OKRs with business reviews?

Answer: Align OKRs with business priorities, establish a consistent review schedule, include cross-functional teams in review sessions, and use data from OKRs to drive discussions and decision-making.

Sample Kpis For Kra Tracking

KPIs that can be used across various areas of organizational management to help in setting and tracking Key Results:

1. Financial KPIs

Revenue Growth
Net Profit Margin
Gross Profit Margin
Operating Income
EBITDA (Earnings Before Interest, Taxes, Depreciation, and Amortization)
Return on Investment (ROI)
Return on Assets (ROA)
Return on Equity (ROE)
Cash Flow
Current Ratio
Quick Ratio
Debt to Equity Ratio
Days Sales Outstanding (DSO)
Days Payable Outstanding (DPO)
Accounts Receivable Turnover
Accounts Payable Turnover
Inventory Turnover
Capital Expenditure (CapEx)
Budget Variance
Economic Value Added (EVA)

2. Customer KPIs

Net Promoter Score (NPS)
Customer Satisfaction Score (CSAT)
Customer Retention Rate
Customer Churn Rate
Customer Lifetime Value (CLTV)

Customer Acquisition Cost (CAC)
Average Revenue Per User (ARPU)
First Contact Resolution (FCR)
Customer Effort Score (CES)
Repeat Purchase Rate

3. Operational KPIs

Operational Efficiency Ratio
Process Cycle Time
Order Fulfillment Time
On-Time Delivery Rate
Production Downtime
Overall Equipment Effectiveness (OEE)
Supply Chain Cycle Time
Cost Per Unit
First Pass Yield (FPY)
Scrap Rate

4. Employee KPIs

Employee Engagement Score
Employee Satisfaction Index
Employee Retention Rate
Employee Turnover Rate
Absenteeism Rate
Training Completion Rate
Time to Hire
Time to Productivity
Internal Promotion Rate
Employee Net Promoter Score (eNPS)

5. Marketing KPIs

Marketing Qualified Leads (MQLs)
Sales Qualified Leads (SQLs)
Cost Per Lead (CPL)
Conversion Rate
Click-Through Rate (CTR)

Customer Acquisition Cost (CAC)
Return on Marketing Investment (ROMI)
Website Traffic
Social Media Engagement
Brand Awareness

6. Sales KPIs

Sales Growth
Sales Target Achievement
Average Deal Size
Sales Cycle Length
Lead Conversion Rate
Win Rate
Sales per Representative
Customer Meeting Rate
Quota Attainment
Upsell and Cross-sell Rates

7. Product Development KPIs

Time to Market
Number of New Products Launched
Product Defect Rate
R&D Spend as a Percentage of Sales
Innovation Index
Feature Adoption Rate
Product Return Rate
Customer Feedback Score
Product Usage Rate
Bug Fix Rate

8. IT and Technology KPIs

System Uptime
Mean Time to Repair (MTTR)
Mean Time Between Failures (MTBF)
IT Support Ticket Resolution Time
IT Support Ticket Volume

Security Incident Rate

Cost Per IT Incident

User Satisfaction with IT Services

Software Deployment Frequency

Percentage of Projects Delivered on Time

9. Environmental and Social Responsibility KPIs

Carbon Footprint

Energy Consumption

Water Usage

Waste Reduction Rate

Recycling Rate

Corporate Social Responsibility (CSR) Spend

Community Impact Score

Supplier Diversity

Employee Volunteer Hours

Ethical Sourcing Percentage

These KPIs span various functions within an organization, providing a comprehensive set of metrics to help set and track Key Results. They can be tailored to fit the specific goals and objectives of different departments and roles within the company.

Sample Okr Case Studies

1. Setting Objectives and Key Results for a General Life Insurance Company:

(PS: The OKRs need to be developed by proper involvement of all team members and cannot be set apriori and handed over to the respective stakeholder. This is only for illlustration purpose)

Let us define a General Life Insurance Company with the following Purpose vision , mission and Strategic Goals:

Purpose: To provide accessible and affordable no-frills insurance products that empower economically backward segments and underserved communities across India, ensuring financial resilience during their most challenging times.

Vision: To become the leading provider of simplified insurance solutions in India, recognized for our commitment to innovation, customer-centricity, and social impact.

Mission: General Life Assurance Company is dedicated to simplifying the insurance experience by offering straightforward products exclusively through group platforms. We aim to expand our reach rapidly, forging strategic partnerships and leveraging existing networks to enhance accessibility and affordability.

Overall Strategy: General Life Assurance Company's strategy revolves around:

Market Expansion and Accessibility:

Rapidly increase market penetration by reaching economically backward segments through strategic partnerships with microfinance institutions and expanding our distribution network into underserved areas.

Product Innovation and Simplification:
Continuously innovate and launch new no-frills insurance products tailored to the specific needs of our target demographics, ensuring simplicity and ease of access.

Operational Efficiency and Customer Experience:
Streamline operational processes to reduce onboarding and claims settlement times, enhancing overall customer experience and satisfaction.

Employee Engagement and Organizational Culture:
Foster a culture of innovation, collaboration, and social responsibility among our employees, ensuring high engagement and alignment with our mission and values.

Sustainability and Social Impact:
Integrate sustainable practices into our business operations and corporate social responsibility initiatives, aiming to make a positive impact on the communities we serve.

Through these strategic initiatives, General Life Assurance Company aims to achieve sustainable growth, operational excellence, and significant social impact in the insurance sector in India.

<u>**Sample OKRs for the above company can be summarised as follows:**</u>

Comprehensive set of OKRs for General Life Assurance Company, including objectives for the leadership and strategic management team, and specifying the level of each OKR:

Strategic Objective 1: Expand Reach and Impact of No-Frills Insurance Products

Objective Owner: Sales and Marketing Team
Key Results:
OKR Level: Company

Objective: Achieve 1 million policies issued within 1 year.

Key Result Owner: Head of Sales

Measure: Number of policies issued

Target: 1,000,000 policies

Timeline: By [Date]

OKR Level: Company

Objective: Increase policy issuance by 200% annually for 5 years.

Key Result Owner: Sales Operations Manager

Measure: Annual growth rate in policies issued

Target: 200% growth year-over-year

Timeline: Annually for 5 years

Strategic Objective 2: Simplify Customer Journey and Claim Settlement Process

Objective Owner: Customer Experience and Operations Team

Key Results:

OKR Level: Departmental

Objective: Reduce onboarding time for new members by 30%.

Key Result Owner: Head of Customer Experience

Measure: Average time to onboard a new member

Target: 30% reduction

Timeline: By [Date]

OKR Level: Departmental

Objective: Innovate claim settlement process to reduce average settlement time to 7 days.

Key Result Owner: Claims Manager

Measure: Average time taken to settle a claim

Target: 7 days

Timeline: By [Date]

Strategic Objective 3: Strengthen Partnerships and Scale Distribution Network

Objective Owner: Business Development and Partnerships Team

Key Results:

OKR Level: Company

Objective: Establish partnerships with 50 new microfinance institutions (MFIs).

Key Result Owner: Head of Partnerships

Measure: Number of new partnerships established

Target: 50 partnerships

Timeline: By [Date]

OKR Level: Company

Objective: Expand distribution network to 500 new locations in underserved areas.

Key Result Owner: Distribution Manager

Measure: Number of new locations opened

Target: 500 new locations

Timeline: By [Date]

Strategic Objective 4: Enhance Product Accessibility and Affordability

Objective Owner: Product Development and Pricing Team

Key Results:

OKR Level: Departmental

Objective: Launch 3 new no-frills insurance products tailored for economically backward segments.

Key Result Owner: Head of Product Development

Measure: Number of new products launched

Target: 3 new products

Timeline: By [Date]

OKR Level: Departmental

Objective: Reduce average premium cost by 20% across all products.

Key Result Owner: Pricing Manager

Measure: Average premium cost per policy

Target: 20% reduction

Timeline: By [Date]

Leadership and Strategic Management OKRs:

OKR Level: Leadership Team

Objective: Foster a culture of innovation and collaboration across all departments.

Key Results:Increase in employee engagement scores by 15% in annual surveys.

Key Result Owner: HR Director

Measure: Employee engagement survey scores

Target: 15% increase

Timeline: By [Date]

Objective: Develop and implement a sustainability strategy to align with corporate social responsibility goals.

Key Results:Launch two new sustainability initiatives.

Key Result Owner: Sustainability Manager

Measure: Number of new initiatives launched

Target: 2 initiatives

Timeline: By [Date]

These OKRs for General Life Assurance Company outline specific objectives, assign ownership to relevant teams or individuals, and specify the level (company-wide or departmental) for each objective and key result. This structure ensures alignment with strategic goals across different levels of the organization.

2. OKR for a Web3 Development Company to launch its Decentralised Application

OKR framework for launching the DApp:

Purpose Strategy, Vision, and Mission

Objective: Define Purpose, Vision, and Mission

Key Result 1 (KR1): Draft and finalize the purpose statement, vision statement, and mission statement for the DApp project by [specific date].Initiatives:

1.1 Conduct brainstorming sessions with core team members and stakeholders.

1.2 Gather input from market research and user insights.

1.3 Develop drafts of purpose, vision, and mission statements.

1.4 Refine statements based on feedback from leadership and stakeholders.

Assigned Responsibilities:

Strategy Lead (SL): Responsible for overseeing the development and alignment of purpose, vision, and mission statements.

Business Analyst (BA): Conducts market research and gathers user insights to inform statement development.

Project Manager (PM): Facilitates brainstorming sessions, coordinates feedback collection, and ensures timelines are met.

Strategy Leadership OKR

Objective: Develop and Execute Strategy for DApp Launch

Key Result 2 (KR2): Define strategic objectives and key results (OKRs) for the DApp launch project by [specific date].Initiatives:

2.1 Analyze market opportunities and competitive landscape.

2.2 Identify strategic partnerships and alliances.

2.3 Outline growth strategies and user acquisition tactics.

2.4 Establish KPIs and success metrics for tracking progress.

Assigned Responsibilities:

Strategy Lead (SL): Accountable for defining strategic objectives and aligning them with overall project goals.

Business Analyst (BA): Assists in market analysis and identification of strategic opportunities.

Legal Team (Legal): Ensures strategic initiatives comply with regulatory requirements.

Marketing Team (Mktg): Develops strategies for user acquisition and promotion aligned with strategic goals.

DApp Launch Process OKR

Objective: Successfully Launch the DApp

Key Result 3 (KR3): Develop and execute a comprehensive roadmap for DApp development and launch by [specific date].Initiatives:

3.1 Create a detailed project timeline and milestone plan.

3.2 Allocate resources and assign roles and responsibilities.

3.3 Conduct regular progress reviews and adjust plans as needed.

3.4 Prepare contingency plans for potential risks and challenges.

Assigned Responsibilities:

Project Manager (PM): Responsible for overall project execution, timeline adherence, and risk management.

Technical Lead (TL): Oversees technical development and ensures alignment with project milestones.

Development Team (Dev): Implements DApp features according to specifications and timeline.

Marketing Team (Mktg): Executes promotional activities and coordinates launch events.

Iterative Improvement OKR

Objective: Iterate and Improve DApp Based on Feedback

Key Result 4 (KR4): Gather user feedback and iterate on DApp features and user experience within the first 6 months post-launch.Initiatives:

4.1 Implement feedback collection mechanisms (surveys, user interviews, etc.).

4.2 Analyze user data and identify areas for improvement.

4.3 Prioritize and implement feature updates and enhancements.

4.4 Measure impact on user satisfaction and engagement metrics.

Assigned Responsibilities:

Product Manager (PM): Leads the product development roadmap based on user feedback and data analysis.

User Experience (UX) Designer: Iterates on DApp design and usability improvements.

Development Team (Dev): Implements updates and enhancements to the DApp based on prioritized features.

Customer Support Team: Provides insights into user feedback and satisfaction levels.

Financial and Operational Management OKR

Objective: Ensure Financial and Operational Stability

Key Result 5 (KR5): Achieve financial sustainability and operational efficiency within the first year of launch.Initiatives:

5.1 Monitor and optimize financial performance metrics (revenue, expenses, ROI).

5.2 Implement cost-saving measures and resource allocation efficiencies.

5.3 Conduct regular financial audits and compliance checks.

5.4 Strengthen partnerships and revenue streams to support long-term growth.

Assigned Responsibilities:

Finance Manager (FM): Manages budgeting, financial reporting, and auditing processes.

Operations Manager (OM): Ensures operational efficiency and scalability of DApp infrastructure.

Legal Team (Legal): Provides oversight on regulatory compliance and risk management.

Business Development (BD): Explores new revenue opportunities and strategic partnerships.

This structured OKR framework assigns clear responsibilities to relevant roles, ensuring alignment with strategic objectives and facilitating effective execution throughout the DApp launch process. Adjustments can be made based on specific team dynamics and project requirements.

Quotes About Okr

OKRs can foster a culture of achievement, innovation, and strategic alignment that leads to organizational growth and success.

John Doerr:

"Ideas are easy. Execution is everything. It takes a team to win. And it takes OKRs to focus that team."

"OKRs have helped countless organizations achieve greatness by focusing efforts on what truly matters and driving alignment towards ambitious goals."

Andy Grove:

"Effective use of OKRs can transform a company's ability to execute and innovate, paving the way for sustained growth and market leadership."

"In the end, the key to a successful implementation of OKRs is to ensure that they become a regular part of the company's operating rhythm."

Larry Page:

"OKRs encourage teams to think big and take risks, which are essential for driving innovation and staying ahead in a rapidly changing world."

"If you're not failing some of the time, you're not pushing yourself hard enough. And that's a big problem in a world where the pace of change is going to continue to accelerate."

Sergey Brin:

"By setting clear objectives and measurable results, OKRs enable teams to prioritize effectively and achieve breakthrough results that propel organizational success."

"Setting ambitious goals can yield unexpected results. It forces you to think differently, to take risks, and see opportunities where others see none."

Christine Wodtke:

"OKRs create a culture of accountability and focus, empowering teams to achieve extraordinary outcomes and drive continuous improvement."

"OKRs are a powerful tool for making sure you're focusing on the right things. They ensure that everyone is moving in the same direction."

These quotes encapsulate the essence of OKRs as a tool for focus, alignment, and driving meaningful progress within organizations.

Glossary

A

Accountability:
The obligation of an individual or team to account for their activities, accept responsibility, and disclose results in a transparent manner.

Alignment:
The process of ensuring all teams and individuals within an organization are working towards the same goals and objectives.

Annual Objectives:
Long-term goals set for a year, providing strategic direction and focus for the organization.

B

Balanced Scorecard:
A strategic planning and management system used to align business activities to the vision and strategy of the organization, improve internal and external communications, and monitor organizational performance against strategic goals.

C

Cadence:
The regular rhythm of OKR planning, review, and update cycles within an organization.

Cascading:
A top-down approach to goal setting where objectives are set at the highest level and then passed down to lower levels. This contrasts with alignment, where objectives are coordinated across levels.

CFR (Conversation, Feedback, Recognition):
A framework within OKR that emphasizes continuous

conversations, feedback loops, and recognition to ensure the alignment and motivation of teams.

CEO (Chief Executive Officer): The highest-ranking executive in a company, responsible for making major corporate decisions, managing overall operations, and setting the strategic direction.

Check-in: A periodic meeting or review session within an organization aimed at tracking progress and discussing the alignment of Objectives and Key Results (OKRs).

D

Dashboard: A visual representation tool used to track the status and progress of OKRs, providing real-time data and insights.

E

Effort: The specific actions and activities undertaken to achieve desired outcomes and objectives.

Execution: The process of carrying out plans and strategies to achieve defined objectives and goals.

F

Focus: The concentration of effort and resources on the most important objectives to ensure significant progress and impact.

Functional Heads: Leaders of specific departments or functions within an organization, responsible for setting and achieving functional objectives.

G

Goal Setting: The process of defining specific, measurable, achievable, relevant, and time-bound objectives to guide organizational efforts.

H

Horizontal Alignment:

The alignment of objectives and efforts across different departments or teams within an organization to ensure cohesive action towards common goals.

I

Implementation Head:

The individual responsible for leading and managing the implementation of the OKR framework within an organization.

Initiatives:

Specific projects or actions undertaken to achieve key results and objectives.

Integration:

The process of combining and coordinating different systems, processes, or tools to work together within the OKR framework.

K

KPI (Key Performance Indicator):

A measurable value that demonstrates how effectively an organization is achieving key business objectives.

KRA (Key Result Area):

The main areas in which an individual or team must achieve results to meet their objectives and contribute to thc overall goals of the organization.

Key Results:

Specific, measurable outcomes that indicate the achievement of an objective.

L

Leadership:

The act of guiding and directing individuals or teams to achieve goals and objectives, often associated with senior executives and managers.

M

Metrics:
Quantifiable measures used to track and assess the status of a specific process or activity within the OKR framework.

Milestones:
Significant points or events in the progress of an objective, often used to measure progress and guide efforts.

N

Non-Measurable Key Results:
Qualitative outcomes that contribute to achieving an objective but are not easily quantified.

O

Objective:
A clear, concise statement of what an organization, team, or individual wants to achieve within a specific time frame.

OKR (Objective and Key Results):
A goal-setting framework used to define and track objectives and their outcomes, ensuring alignment and engagement across the organization.

OKR Program Management Head:
The individual responsible for the overall adoption and success of the OKR initiative within the company.

OKR Program Management Manager:
The individual responsible for executing the plans to implement OKRs successfully.

P

Performance Management System (PMS):
A framework used to evaluate and improve individual and organizational performance through goal-setting, feedback, and reviews.

Program Management Manager:
The individual responsible for executing and managing the

plans and activities to implement OKRs successfully within an organization.

Program Management Head:
The senior executive responsible for overseeing the adoption and integration of the OKR initiative across the organization.

Q

Quality Outcomes:
The successful achievement of objectives through effective planning and execution, resulting in measurable and impactful results.

R

Review Session:
A regular meeting where progress on OKRs is assessed, challenges are discussed, and adjustments are made to ensure objectives are on track.

S

SMART Goals:
Objectives that are Specific, Measurable, Achievable, Relevant, and Time-bound.

Stretch Goals:
Ambitious, challenging objectives that push teams and individuals beyond their comfort zones to achieve significant progress and breakthroughs.

Strategy:
A high-level plan designed to achieve one or more long-term or overall goals under conditions of uncertainty.

Strategy Head:
An executive responsible for developing and executing the strategic plan of the organization, often involved in leading OKR implementation.

T

Team-Based OKRs:

OKRs set at the team level, focusing on collaborative efforts and shared objectives to enhance teamwork and collective achievement.

Transparency:

The practice of making information available to all stakeholders, fostering openness and trust within the organization.

U

Urgency:

The need for immediate and focused action to achieve objectives and drive organizational progress.

V

Vision:

A clear and inspiring long-term goal that defines the desired future state of the organization.

W

Weekly Check-Ins:

Regular updates on progress towards OKRs, helping to maintain focus and momentum.

Will:

The determination and commitment to achieve set objectives, regardless of obstacles and challenges.

Y

Yearly Objectives:

Long-term goals set for a year, providing strategic direction and focus for the organization.

About The Authors

Vikram Kohli, co-founder of Qilo, an OKR platform acquired by PeopleStrong in 2019, is passionate about unlocking organizational value through strategic alignment. With over 18 years of experience in tech, Vikram has built and scaled tech products, transforming ideas from concepts to realities. His journey began with coding and evolved into leading product development, overcoming multiple startup challenges to achieve success.

Vikram excels in understanding business dynamics, ensuring sustainable growth, and building resilient solutions that scale. He is adept at creating and motivating high-performing teams, fostering an environment that is both productive and enjoyable. His deep expertise in OKRs and strategic execution has made him a thought leader, sharing his knowledge to help organizations achieve their goals and sustain growth. Through speaking engagements, workshops, and publications, Vikram continues to drive organizational excellence and inspire others in the tech and business community.

Srinivas Mahankali, an IIT/IIM alumnus and director at a BSE-listed Cutting Technology company, is a seasoned executive with over 35 years of experience. He co-founded MMAPL, a strategy consulting firm, specializing in aligning strategies for profitable business growth. With a background as a CXO/Director in IT for over 20 years, Mahankali has authored 15+ books on technology and business management, including "Successful Organizations in Action." He's a pioneer in Blockchain and WEB3 technologies, and has implemented frameworks like Balanced Scorecard and OKRs. His leadership in cybersecurity, cloud, and data underscores his role in shaping future-ready organizational strategies.